Government and the Universities in Britain
1960–1980

'That's Genesis ... I suppose you might say we're in Numbers now. And, I'm afraid, getting close to Job and Lamentations.'

– The Vice-Chancellor of Watermouth University, c.1967; in Malcolm Bradbury's *The History Man*, p. 47

GOVERNMENT AND THE UNIVERSITIES IN BRITAIN

Programme and Performance 1960–1980

JOHN CARSWELL

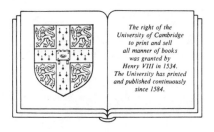

The right of the
University of Cambridge
to print and sell
all manner of books
was granted by
Henry VIII in 1534.
The University has printed
and published continuously
since 1584.

CAMBRIDGE UNIVERSITY PRESS

Cambridge
London   New York   New Rochelle
Melbourne   Sydney

Published by the Press Syndicate of the University of Cambridge
The Pitt Building, Trumpington Street, Cambridge CB2 IRP
32 East 57th Street, New York, NY 10022, USA
10 Stamford Road, Oakleigh, Melbourne 3166, Australia

First published 1985

Printed in Great Britain at The Bath Press, Avon

British Library Cataloguing in Publication Data
Carswell, John, 1918–
Government and the universities in Britain:
programme and performance 1960–80.
1. Universities and colleges—Great Britain—
History–20th century
I. Title
378.41   LA636.8

Library of Congress Cataloging in Publication Data
Carswell, John.
Government and the universities in Britain.
1. Higher education and state–Great Britain—History
—20th century. 2. Universities and colleges—Great
Britain—Finance—History—20th century. I. Title.
LC178.G7C37   1986   379.41   85-12821

ISBN 0 521 25826 X

Errata

p. 71, footnote 4: "With his death" should read "With his resignation."

p. 131, line 10: "about a year later" should read "about three years later."

p. 131, footnote 1: The note should read "Sir Herbert Andrew has spent his career in the Board of Trade. Of his three predecessors, two (Sir John Maud and Dame Mary Smieton) came from outside the Education Department. The exception was Sir Gilbert Flemming (Permanent Secretary 1952-59)."

To all those
in the Universities and Whitehall
who have the handling of these matters
now and in future

Contents

Preface

This book arises from experience which began in 1960 when, at the age of forty-one and a civil servant of thirteen years' standing, I was assigned to a desk in the Treasury which was concerned, among many other things, with the universities. Their expansion was already under way, and the Robbins Committee was just being appointed.

So by a turn of fate most of the rest of my career was spent – though in different alignments – on the border between the state and the universities: first preparing the Treasury's evidence for the Robbins Committee and acting as the Treasury assessor with it; then as the Undersecretary responsible for the university programme in the newly founded Department of Education and Science; and then, after an interval of about six years, as Secretary of the University Grants Committee.

This period of eighteen years very nearly coincided with the period over which the Robbins Committee drew its projection. It therefore constitutes a coherent chapter in the history of the British universities and their relationship with the state, and I personally experienced the transition from a public euphoria, which it was my duty to moderate, to a mood of public disillusionment, against which it was my duty to contend. My first experience was of an almost unstoppable wave of demand on public funds and my last was of a sandy beach with the tide almost out of sight.

The completeness of the period allows a comparison between what was attempted and what was achieved, and suggestions about the reasons why one varied from the other in important respects.

I hope that this, and the narrative of what lay between 1960 and 1978, will give a historical perspective to the present situation.

Most of the resources for this book have been drawn from my own experience and from published documents, which I refer to in foot-notes. I have been much helped by a number of conversations with people who had an important part: Lord Murray of Newhaven, Lord Wolfenden, Sir Frederick Dainton, Sir Herbert Andrew, Sir Toby Weaver, Professor Dame Helen Gardner, Professor Lionel Elvin and Sir Claus Moser. To all of them I owe debt of gratitude, as I do also

Preface

to the Librarian of the University of London Institute of Education, where I did much of my reading, and his staff. My gratitude is also due to the History Department of University College, London, where an honorary research fellowship gave me facilities which were indispensable.

J.P.C.

Hampstead, 1 December 1984

I

The Background

In writing a chapter of university history it is dangerously easy to gener-
alise, even though much of what one intends is an account covering
a period one personally saw and experienced at close quarters.
Universities, in the words of a distinguished Permanent Secretary under
whom I served, are 'a big round subject' and my own relationship
with them, in good times and bad, has been in terms of existing situa-
tions. There has been a personal theme in that relationship, though
I hope it has never interfered with the advice I gave or the decisions
I took. The story as a whole, by chance, forms a complete picture,
so I cannot resist putting in some background, sky and clouds before
I start it: what in the civil service is called 'the context'.

Change and development in universities have to be considered in
terms of lifetimes, because the university experience forms lives. Those
who work on the staff of universities commonly spend their lifetimes
doing so and even those who attend only as students do not usually
forget the experience. My context must therefore start with the time
when I went to university (Oxford) just before the Second World War.

At that time the total number of undergraduates in British universities was scarcely more than the number of full-time university academic
staff today;[1] and one must also allow for polytechnics, which did not
exist as a system in 1937. Education beyond the age of fifteen was
then still privileged, sacrificial, highly competitive; the opportunities
for women in higher studies outside teacher-training colleges were path-
etically sparse; and the demands for scientific manpower were still
in their infancy, even though Jowett, at the end of his life, had drawn
attention to the scientific future of the universities and in 1931 the
atom had been split at the Cavendish Laboratory.

The contrast is surprising even when all allowances are made. A
power ruling half the world needed, or seemed to need, only about
a tenth of the graduates Britain has today. The normal route for an
engineer, an accountant, a solicitor, often a doctor, did not lie through

---

[1] In 1937 the number of university undergraduates was about 48,000. In 1981 the number
of university academic staff was almost 43,000.

the university at all. It was difficult for arts graduates to find jobs. Universities themselves recruited only about a hundred graduates a year to the academic profession.

The universities did not occupy a large place in the consciousness of the nation as a whole, for whom they came to the surface only in sporting events such as the Boat Race – and then it was only Oxford and Cambridge. They were respected landmarks. Between 1918 and 1945 Baldwin was the only Prime Minister to have a university degree, but since 1945 only two (Churchill and Callaghan) have lacked them. True, the universities were represented in Parliament by thirteen members, but they were returned by an electorate of less than 100,000 graduates in contests which rarely involved a party battle and were often undisputed.[2]

The great change in the size and importance of the universities was largely the work of those who had attended them in the decade before the War and of their younger teachers. There were indeed outside, contingent influences: the War itself, and the influx of already qualified refugees (the products of the massive German university expansion of the 1920s) without whom the picture would have been incomparably different, and with whom the universities have moved into an international dimension which has replaced the former imperial role. The universities of the thirties may have been small, but they were lively. Keynes published the *General Theory* in 1936, Namier began to revolutionise the writing of history in 1930. Cambridge had Leavis, Eddington, Thomson, Quiller-Couch, Gowland Hopkins, Moore and Trevelyan; and had instituted a degree in archaeology and anthropology. Oxford had Tolkien, Beazley, Lindemann; and had instituted a degree in philosophy, politics and economics. London University acquired a large part of Bloomsbury, built a ziggurat to mark its centre, and in 1929 gained the right from the University Grants Committee (UGC) to distribute a block grant among its constituent colleges.[3]

Despite, or perhaps because of, Britain having proportionately fewer university students than any country in Western Europe (let alone the United States) its universities achieved an extraordinary power over the feelings and outlook of those who studied in them. This was quite unaffected by the revolutionary opinions with which some of those graduates emerged. I have met many of that generation who repudiated

---

[2] If university representation had continued on the same proportions, the electorate would now require about 130 seats in the House of Commons.

[3] *UGC Report for the Period 1929–30 to 1934–35*, HMSO, 1936, p. 9.

their schooldays with horror and disgust, but none – even the most radical – who really wanted to subvert or destroy the university world he had known. This affection for universities, the sense of having acquired values by which to live, was to be most important in what happened later.

This sense of a world which was small, beautiful and detached, though bearing no relation to reality, has extraordinary power and endurance for both the lovers of universities and their critics. I have never been able to find the origin of the cliché 'ivory tower', which expresses one (usually hostile) approach to this.[4]

In 1937 there were twenty-one universities (including the five just emerging from the ambiguous status of university colleges) as against forty-four today.[5] Three-quarters of the students were at seven of the institutions: London, Oxford, Cambridge and four ancient universities of Scotland (Glasgow, Edinburgh, Aberdeen and St Andrews). Indeed London had a quarter, Oxford and Cambridge a quarter between them and Scotland another quarter.

The other 12,500 students were thus spread over fourteen institutions, many of which were smaller than a major college in London or Cambridge, and for these the useful term 'redbrick' came into use.[6] They were predominantly in the northern half of England, where civic pride and old industrial money had placed them. Though they had senates charged with academic authority they were not self-governing

---

[4] Bacon, in his *Advancement of Learning*, speaks of 'a tower of state for a proud mind to raise itself upon', and Vergil (*Aeneid* vi, 893–6) of two *gates* to the underworld, one of horn and the other of ivory. The first provides a passage for reliable thoughts, the second for vain imaginations and illusions:

> *Sunt geminae Somni portae, quarum altera fertur*
> *cornea, qua veris facilis datur exitus umbris,*
> *altera candenti perfecta nitens elephanto,*
> *sed falsa ad caelum mittunt insomnia manes.*

Perhaps Vergil was prophesying binarism.

[5] Counting universities is a specialised art. I have here followed the practice of the UGC, which I will explain later. (See Appendix III.) The 'redbricks' of the pre-war system were Birmingham, Bristol, Durham, Leeds, Liverpool, Manchester, Reading and Sheffield (all full universities) and the emerging university colleges of Exeter, Hull, Leicester, Nottingham and Southampton: plus the University of Wales with its widely separated and semi-autonomous colleges, then five in number.

[6] The term 'redbrick' appears in the title of the book *Redbrick University* by 'Bruce Truscot' (Faber, 1943), which is an eloquent plea for the civic universities of England, 'which are all very much the same type – a type which, if it can be modified in ways shortly to be suggested, will probably dominate English university education in centuries to come. Their foundation is due to local effort; their endowments come largely from local pockets; they are aided by grants from local municipal activities; and their students, though to a slowly decreasing extent, are drawn from local areas' (p. 16).

corporations of scholars like Oxford and Cambridge. Financial and administrative responsibility lay with a council on which local lay interests were strongly represented; and day-to-day management was in the hands of a permanent Vice-Chancellor appointed by the council. The 'redbrick' Vice-Chancellor was thus very far from being the short-term chairman of an academic corporation, though one of his duties was to preside in the senate. He was the permanent head of the administration.

The larger civic universities – those of the Midlands and the North – still conformed with the intentions of their founders by drawing most of their students from their own neighbourhoods.[7] It was not unnatural for local authorities to pay quite generously for students attending such universities, and when the rare chance of a place for a member of one of their own families came up at London, Oxford or Cambridge, admiring ratepayers would admit the charge. After all, were not the civic universities supported in many other ways by the local community? Had not the University of Wales been built by the pennies of the people? Did not the University College of Nottingham derive a quarter of its income from neighbouring local authorities and much of the rest from the generosity of local employers?

The Welsh and Scottish universities were important symbols of their respective national identities – especially the Welsh. Oxford, Cambridge and London were metropolitan, in the sense of drawing students from all over the country; but they were in addition, and alone, international. There were fewer than 5,000 overseas students in the system altogether. Seventy per cent of them were at either London, Cambridge or Oxford. Edinburgh led among the Scottish universities with about 400. Elsewhere overseas students were numbered in scores, or even dozens, Southampton had six, Cardiff four.

The general outlook of the governments and student bodies of the redbricks might be local: it was quite otherwise with the academic staff, who had for the most part graduated at one of the three metropolitan universities. It was only to be expected. Those universities were older, bigger, grander. In 1935 London had 75 per cent of the graduate students in the whole country; and the three metropolitan universities between them produced far more of those who sought university careers than they could themselves provide for. There was a familiar cursus

[7] In 1935 the five biggest (Leeds, Manchester, Cardiff, Glasgow and Liverpool) contained not quite 12,000 students. Nearly 9,000 had their homes within thirty miles of the university they were attending. *UGC Report 1929–35*, p. 65.

4

honorum for such a graduate: a junior lectureship at a provincial university followed by a return to the metropolis as a college fellow, to end once more in redbrick with a chair.

As a result the metropolitan style pervaded, and was even exaggerated, in the academic life of the provinces. Manners were more formal, discipline stricter, innovation of curriculum less common, eccentricity less acceptable. The same, incidentally, could be said, even in the metropolitans, about the colleges for women. As for medical schools it should be recorded that in 1935 there was not a single woman medical student at Guy's, St Thomas's, St Bartholomew's, Charing Cross, St George's the Middlesex or St Mary's.

For all its apparent placidity the university system of the thirties contained a dynamism that was to determine future events. This lay in the tension between the metropolitan and the provincial institutions – penetrated as these had been by the academic standards and memories which had come to them from the older universities. The institutional urge to expand did not originate in Oxford, Cambridge or even London – though all quickly sensed the necessity to fall in with it. The steam was generated in the redbrick universities.

So far, though, I have been discussing the universities as a system of institutions – the way the UGC, for instance, has traditionally seen them. But there is a point of view from which universities appear as no more than the administrative and financial shells within which scholarship and research are carried on. The naming, description and invention of subjects are not initiated by universities, though they may be blessed by them. It is true that they are reflected gradually by the internal organisation of universities into faculties and departments; true also that there is a university pride and loyalty towards a successful or traditional subject. But the organic world of the universities consists of those with similar interests, wherever they are located in the system. It does not consist so much of universities, faculties and departments as of historians, physicists and economists; of Tudor historians, solid-state physicists and econometricians. These create their own formal and informal associations within which cooperation and rivalry develop. It is within them that a career develops or fails. Competition for funds (or survival) is within the university framework, but competition for recognition is within the subject. This aspect touches on what is known now as the 'dual support system'.

But there is yet a third way of looking at the system, even at the modest size I have described, which is neither that of an official administering grants to institutions nor of an academic working in the system itself. Those who write about universities do not often include it, but it has considerable influence on university policy at every level. This is simply to consider universities as corporations in the economy: as employers of labour, as purchasers of goods and services, as businesses attracting private and (in increasing quantities) public money to particular localities. Even in the 1930s Cambridge, Durham, St Andrews and Aberystwyth had their biggest employer in the shape of a university institution. This gave university administrations, especially in what might be called 'university towns', an importance quite separate from their authority in the university's internal affairs. In this respect universities had some of the characteristics of the great monastic houses of the Middle Ages. And they were not only employers and spenders: they were in many cases (and not only in Oxford and Cambridge) considerable proprietors.

So – not often mentioned, though quickly obvious – universities came to provide a considerable range of services free to all comers in their localities: parks, museums, picture galleries, monuments. Their libraries, especially the two copyright libraries of Oxford and Cambridge, serve a far wider public than the universities. The Courtauld Galleries, the Fitzwilliam, the Ashmolean, the Barber Institute, the Parks at Oxford, the Backs at Cambridge, and much else, give the universities a public and a national character that is taken for granted but cannot be muffled by contrasting them with a 'public sector' as private bodies. Indeed, at the time we are talking about, the idea that a university was a private body would have seemed odd.

The universities selected the student body. From this two consequences followed: there was an implicit contract that the university would use its best offices to ensure a degree, so wastage rates were low; and the student found himself accepting university authority. University authority was often spoken of, and made a great parade. It consisted primarily in academic judgment in terms of marking and classification, and secondarily in a claim over behaviour which had more about it of the mould than of the policeman. The machinery for exerting this latter aspect of authority was almost self-consciously theatrical and antique. The new arrival at Oxford received a copy of the statutes and read with a smile which was at the same time supportive and contemptuous that he should not play marbles on the steps of the Sheldonian Theatre or visit a public house on pain of being amerced or even placed in the Black Book of the Proctors. But he also accepted

6

(even if as something to be secretly evaded) that he should live either in college or in licensed lodgings, to which he must return at stated times, and in which he must not have the company of ladies after six in the evening. The rules applying to women's establishments were even more rigorous, and accepted in the same spirit.

It was the same with the staff. They too had been chosen, by more elaborate processes, with an implied contract of indefinite continuance. The result was independence, variety, eccentricity, occasional degeneration; yet very little by way of effective machinery was needed because the system engendered an almost unquestioning allegiance. The dons of the thirties may have been comfortable, but they worked hard. The ratio of staff to students was about 1:11.

Universities, like other independent organisations, have always had the right of self-description in every respect, and those who discuss them are equally free to categorise in the way that suits them. The UGC eventually arrived at a categorisation of seventeen subjects – very properly a prime number – and social science was detached from 'arts' as a major grouping in 1961. But in the context of the 1930s arts, pure science, technology, medicine and the modest rural miscellany clustering round agriculture were the recognised divisions statistically.

Medical education, when I was Secretary of the University Grants Committee, absorbed about a quarter of the whole university grant: an answer, if any were needed, to those who talk of 'ivory towers'. Somehow, just the same, it is not usually brought into education discussion. Its scale is the affair of the Health Ministry, not the Education Ministry, and its products move into a professional world which itself plays a great part in educating its recruits. Even within the university, medical schools follow a different rhythm, working through the year with a short holiday, and not in terms divided by vacations. Many of the teachers practise the profession, and the name of hospital, rather than the name of the university, traditionally sets the mark on the student. Moreover the teachers are for the most part paid more – whence the strange description of the scales approved from time to time for all other university staff as 'non-clinical'.

Science was already the growth point, though the bud was still small: so small that it is not easy to see at once how this country's scientific reputation could have been established on so narrow a base. In the mid-thirties there were about 9,000 science students in what the UGC then described as 'Pure Science', and about 4,500 in technology – a total of 13,000 or so, and about a quarter of the university population.

Of the 4,500 technology students less than a hundred were women. Cambridge, which had recently launched engineering, had no women in the subject. Imperial College had two, among 519 men.

It is possible to speculate that only the infusion of fully trained scientists created by the German university expansion of the twenties and driven westwards by Hitlerite persecution gave the necessary broadening to the base.

This introduces a broad general point which had great importance in what happened later, namely the immense emphasis which is always placed in discussions about British universities on the concept of a 'full-time student': by which is meant a person who has no commitment except to study, as distinct from a person whose studies only form part of other commitments – perhaps to job, perhaps to a home. These are 'part-time' students, and by a kind of instinct of the English language 'full-time' is conceived as more convincing than 'part-time', as if one were 'professional', the other 'amateur'. Yet the intensity of concentration at the time of study is no less for one than for another, nor are the qualifications aimed for (and mostly attained) less valuable. Universities, however, on the whole treated 'full-time' as the core, 'part-time' as the worthy margin. The reason is understandable: the full-time student is a full-time member of the community and the corporation that constitutes the university.

The connection between what has just been said and the reinforcement of British science and scholarship by the refugees from Hitlerite Europe is simply this. The effective skill of a community is more rapidly raised by the injection of skilled and qualified people who have already made progress in a career, than it is by training the young. This is not only because the training of the young takes time, but because the young person arrives with his qualification at a junior level from which it is difficult to influence matters. The older qualified person is more likely to be able to apply the influence of his skill with immediate effect. Evidence for this can be supplied from English history not only from the Jewish immigrations of the 1930s but from the Huguenot immigrations of three centuries ago. The factor is also important in the rapid economic development of the United States; and strongly reinforces the usefulness of adult education programmes.

Until the great upheavals that began about 1960 the arts were the core of university studies. Half the students in 1935 were in arts faculties. The picture was even more sharply marked at the universities of Oxford and Cambridge, whose arts students constituted respectively

8

80 per cent and 70 per cent of the entire student number.[8] Philosophy, history, law, economics, the subjects relating to what humanity had done rather than the eternity it explored, dominated their outlook.

The arts were therefore central. Not only were they located most strongly in the ancient, beautiful and big universities – they were the stock from which all the other branches of study had grown. Their claim as direct contributors to material wellbeing might be feeble, but the very idea of a university, being an idea, was in their custody. Their view of themselves was confirmed by public opinion and the strange shadow which past public opinion casts over the present. The typical university teacher, even today, is not thought of by the man in the street as a chemist or a surgeon, but as an historian or a philosopher.

Despite occasional royal and governmental interventions[9] the British universities are not emanations of the state, though in a way they form part of it. Constitutionally speaking they and their components are and always have been (even when brought into existence by the will of the state) self-governing corporations with their own incomes and property, employing their own staff and choosing their own students. But that they should not be part of the state, like universities in all major countries except the United States and Japan, is in the broadest sense impossible. The qualifications they offer, their influence on the whole system of education, and above all the inevitable influence of their graduates in every field over long periods, cannot fail to make them public institutions. It is not possible, and never has been, to draw a distinction which will stand the test of time between the universities and a 'state system of higher education'.

Two characteristics distinguished the British universities of the 1930s from most other universities in the world and have become engrained with important consequences. As their primary qualification (indeed in the thirties it was thought of as almost the only qualification)[10] the universities offered a degree (achieved after three, or at most four, years' intensive study) to students they themselves chose; and they held themselves out as the main centres of research over the whole

[8] In London only one-third of the students were in arts faculties, in Manchester less than half, at Leeds just over a third, at Edinburgh less than half.
[9] E.g. King James II's dispute with Magdalen College, Oxford, the Whig Government's quartering of cavalry on Oxford in 1720, the founding of the Regius chairs at Oxford and Cambridge, the nineteenth-century Royal Commissions on the universities, and the Scottish Universities Act 1889.
[10] The BA or its equivalent. The PhD had been introduced in the 1920s on the German model, primarily to attract students from abroad.

range of learning. These two fundamental features had two implications: the intending student had to reach what would now be considered a very advanced level before admission[11] and staffing was on a basis that provided for intensive teaching and for a margin of research.

From 1919 onwards the direct contribution of the state to the universities was distributed through the University Grants Committee. Its origins lie with an able civil servant of the Board of Education named A. H. Kidd, who became the first Secretary of the agency he had created. His problem was to reconcile the need for the Exchequer to subsidise universities as a national system with the need to maintain the autonomy of the universities as indispensable for the function they performed. The distribution of the subsidy (in whatever measure the Treasury made available) was thus placed in the hands of a body of eminent persons whose decisions on distribution would not, by convention, ever be questioned.

Since its foundation the UGC has gone through several clearly distinguishable phases, even though it is, even today, formally what was created in 1919: a committee nominated by the Government to advise it on the quantum of state support to be given to universities as a whole, and to distribute between the different institutions whatever amount the Government might decide upon after considering that advice. The first of these functions was in the strictest sense advisory and the Government was in no way obliged to accept the Committee's advice on it. The second – the distributive function – was and always has been executive. The subtlety of this arrangement lay in devolving that executive responsibility to a Treasury committee served by Treasury officials in such a way that, although Treasury control was retained, political and parliamentary questions did not enter into the delicate issues involved.

The Whitehall context in which this happened was very different from what it later became. At that time the Treasury was not, except at moments of crisis, seen as the department with overall responsibility for the regulation of the economy or even of the planning of public expenditure. As the budgetary department it was responsible for scrutinising all expenditure proposals, but it also spent a great deal itself for a variety of purposes, including science and what is now known as the arts. There was nothing unusual, therefore, in its making direct

---

[11] An applicant in history was expected to have read the whole of Gibbon and Macaulay; in English most of Shakespeare, Milton, Fielding and Jane Austen; in classics most of Vergil, Homer and Horace, and at least some of the Greek dramatists.

grants to the universities, especially when one considers how very small these grants were.

They were not only small in themselves – even by the mid-thirties they were only some £2m a year – but they were barely a third of total university income, the rest being made up from fees, endowments, and (very important) grants from local authorities. Not a single university was receiving as much as half its income from the UGC in 1935. The most dependent was St Andrews, which got 46.3 per cent of its income in UGC grant. The Manchester College of Technology got only 9.8 per cent.

This fact in itself put the universities beyond the reach of parliamentary audit and the ministrations of the Comptroller and Auditor General, whose entrée is limited to institutions receiving more than half their income from the Exchequer. Only when this fraction was exceeded did any special defence from parliamentary audit have to be mounted.

Since all payments to universities continued to be made by the Treasury Accountant (though on the UGC's instructions) they were still open to audit; but why they were what they were was a matter of judgment and policy, not administrative or financial propriety, and so was outside the scope of the Comptroller and Auditor General. In brief the UGC had no accounts to audit.

Nevertheless the officials of the UGC were financial officials, not educational administrators. Their main task was to calculate grant on what was known as 'the deficiency principle' – in other words to apply a needs test to each institution on the grant list in terms of money. After estimating the very important fraction of each university's income that came from other sources, and its anticipated expenditure on the assumption that everything remained as it was, the difference was taken as each university's basic need. To the extent that a university was contemplating some development which the Committee was willing to accept as desirable, a contribution towards its cost would then be added; but such developments in the thirties were small and rare. The needs thus assembled were then added together as advice on the total grant for the coming quinquennium and then used as the basis for the distribution of whatever total was finally agreed by the Treasury.

The five-year cycle required for this operation gave birth to a peculiar characteristic of the Committee, which marked it out from all other advisory bodies and gave it a special atmosphere of its own. It decided corporately to visit each of its institutions and spend a day or two there every five years forming its impressions of the university's work and future and giving its advice. These visitations have often been criticised as stilted and superficial, but they did have the effect of concentrating minds in each university from time to time on its operations as a whole, and gave the UGC itself a quasi-collegiate coherence derived from its members and officers travelling and living together for a perceptible part of their lives, something they would not have developed from regular meetings in a London committee-room.

The UGC thus developed a personality of its own, and in the eyes of its officials became a kind of collective Minister. Naturally, in the way of officials, they came to claim the exclusive right to advise this 'collective Minister' in confidence, and accordingly obtained exclusive control over all papers and discussions in which that advice was generated. They would allow no contact with the committee from which they were excluded, and no discussions between any part of Whitehall and the universities without their being aware of it first. This bureaucratic fortification of the UGC's independence was every bit as important as the independence and eminence of its membership. It was under no obligation to reveal its hand till it was ready to declare it.

Yet even as it developed these characteristics the UGC was not *under* the Treasury. It was part of it. Its work was financial. Its secretariat consisted of Treasury officials constituting a kind of specialised division of the Treasury working within a specific budgetary authority. It freely consulted other Treasury divisions where their interests were involved. It attended Treasury Ministers when university questions arose.

I have entered into the early history of the UGC in some detail, not only because the UGC plays a great part in this narrative, but to demonstrate one important conclusion. The UGC was invented as a device in recognition of the autonomy of the universities, which was then financial as well as constitutional; but it was not invented to safeguard it. Only by the force of history did it acquire an aura of principles and mystique which would have astonished its founders.

The UGC's inventors could never have foreseen the theological commentary that was to grow up round their modest device. 'I know, I know,' said Sir Maurice Dean in 1964 when it was all put to him by Sir John Wolfenden, 'Clothed in white Samite, mystic, wonderful – I entirely agree.'

In 1937 (for I rushed ahead too far) the UGC was a highly respectable backwater of Whitehall. It consisted of only nine members, including the well-meaning, deeply Christian Chairman, Sir Walter Moberly. Five of the other eight were octogenarians, and none of the Committee except the Chairman was under sixty. The statistics it produced, though quite copious, were amateurish and uninformative, and to our eyes at any rate its attitudes were paternalistic, sentimental and rooted in tradition.

Yet under the complacent rhetoric of its reports the problems of the future are already perceptible: the danger of unrestrained development leading to duplication of effort; scepticism about research;[12] uneasiness about the market for graduates. And the banner of the Committee carried at least one battle honour. During the economic crisis of 1931 the Chairman of the UGC (then Sir Walter Buchanan Riddell) had bidden defiance to the Treasury and the cuts imposed by the May Committee. Shooting grouse in Scotland in the September of that eventful year Sir Walter received a telegram to say his current year's grant was to be reduced. From that very moor – so he told the Committee when it reassembled – he sent a reply that such a thing was unthinkable, and that the most he could forego was the modest reserve built up from previous years for future development; and he won. The universities escaped the cuts that caused the naval mutiny at Invergordon.

For the first twenty years of its existence the University Grants Committee dispensed the grants made available to it in support of institutions, which were expanding very gently, if at all. Nobody except professionals cared very much about university finance. No new institutions came into existence. There was no strong sense that the blessings of higher education should be made more widely available as an act of Government policy, or that scientific and technical change would create a national need for qualified manpower on a vastly greater scale. Although UGC grant had long been indispensable to the existence of even the richest universities, it did not, as we have seen, constitute more than half the income of any of the institutions. The UGC was there to see that the grant did not exceed reasonable bounds and was properly administered. In no other sense was it an instrument of Government policy. Nor, in general, was it called upon to intervene with the Government on behalf of the universities.

Once the War was over the Treasury decided to invigorate the formerly placid scene. The UGC's terms of reference requiring it to inquire

[12] 'Much of what is now called research does not necessarily advance knowledge, and there is some danger lest the word itself should lose the dignity which ought to attach to it' (*UGC Report 1929–35*, p. 34).

into needs, distribute the grant and publish information were enlarged by the addition of these fateful words:

and to assist, in consultation with the universities and other bodies concerned, the preparation and execution of such plans for the development of the universities as may from time to time be required in order to ensure that they are fully adequate to national needs.

What is more, the small group of elder statesmen was tactfully moved into retirement and replaced by a much larger committee in which working academics constituted the majority.[13] The chairmanship was put on a full-time basis with the status of a Third Secretary.

The result of this quiet measure of nationalisation was not immediately apparent. But that part of the income of universities which came from sources other than grant had been much diminished by wartime inflation. From 1946 onwards the UGC grant was not only indispensable to the universities: it constituted the greater part of their income. The parliamentary Committee of Public Accounts therefore embarked on its long and ultimately successful campaign to subject the expenditure of both the UGC and the universities to parliamentary scrutiny.

In 1953 Sir Keith Murray (now Lord Murray of Newhaven) was appointed Chairman of the UGC and presided over the development of the universities for the next ten years. The effects of his period in office, though little noticed outside the university world, can hardly be exaggerated. In manner large, benevolent, persuasive, in action almost inexhaustible, he was a convinced and consistent expansionist. He was no delegator. Provided he had facts and figures he could draft a blue-book of 200 pages singlehanded in a matter of weeks. He was a man for the times.[14]

Between 1935 and 1961 the number of university students more than doubled – from 51,000 to 113,000 – with undertakings that it would go very much higher (I include postgraduates. Unless the context otherwise requires, all the student figures I give include postgraduate, but exclude part-time students). In 1956, his third year of chairmanship, Murray's capital programme was £3.8m: for 1963, his last, it

---

[13] For further detail see Chapter VII.
[14] It would be wrong not to mention that during the earlier part of his chairmanship he was supported by one of the ablest men to serve as Secretary of the UGC, Sir Edward Hale. Hale was the first senior professional administrator to apply his mind to university needs and university costs. He was the first to identify, and begin planning for, the wave of demand for university education which was set up by the Education Act of 1944 and the dramatic rise in the birth rate following the War. His period of office at the UGC was from 1953 to 1958.

was £30.0m with a promise that it would be still more. No fewer than seven new universities emerged during his chairmanship after personal visits by him to numerous sites proposed by local interests. In addition Dundee was severed from St Andrews, Newcastle from Durham, adding two more to the number of universities. The ancient and thorny problem of Lampeter was resolved and it became, despite its Anglican origins, an additional college of the nonconformist University of Wales. But perhaps the most significant achievement of all, considered socially, was his creation of a national system for application to the universities for intending students. It involved some cession of total autonomy by the institutions, and on that account alone was remarkable. Without UCCA a university system on a national scale matched to opportunity would have been grossly inefficient, probably impossible.

The Treasury accepted, indeed it sympathised with, this forward policy. It defended the UGC and the universities from the increasingly acid demands of the Public Accounts Committee to have access to the details of what was happening. But it was becoming uncomfortable about the traffic through what other departments subjected to Treasury scrutiny regarded as a private door.

II

The Treasury

When I arrived in the Treasury in January 1960 the general atmosphere was that of a besieged garrison. The division of which I found myself second in command contained about the same number of staff as the one from which I had just come in the Ministry of Pensions and National Insurance; but it was responsible for the control of all social service expenditure: national insurance, national assistance, health, housing and local government, education, the Medical Research Council and the universities. It also included the rating of Government property and peculiar functions such as approval of the rates of Gibraltar (they were always the same, and seemed to be remarkably low), the distribution of haunches of venison culled from the Royal Parks, and the appointment of the Keeper of the Physic Garden.

My immediate chief was a gentle, hard-working, dying man: J. A. C. Robertson. On his sick-bed he read files and from it sent urgent messages. He came to the office almost on the day of his death, which happened about a year after I arrived. Above him, as Third Secretary presiding over the whole of public expenditure, was Richard Clarke. 'Otto', as he was universally known, had had a brilliant career at Cambridge, where he had read mathematics, and had first made his mark as a financial journalist, in which capacity he is said to have devised the *Financial Times* share index. His principles had then been socialist, and he had written a book about the nationalisation of the steel industry under the well-chosen pseudonym 'Ingot', which might have served as a very good nickname for him if someone else's inspiration had not made him Otto. Nobody knew why, but Otto he undoubtedly was.

He had some of the characteristics of a high officer on Ludendorff's *Grossgeneralstab*: massive presence, neurotic mannerisms, sparkling intelligence, a rather squeaky voice. A more relentless man I have never met. When he became enthused with a subject his fingers would drum on the table before him and his eyes achieved a strange and compelling brilliance which darted here and there among those he was addressing. He was essentially a man of ideas, all of which seemed to him unquestionably right, so that those who opposed them, once

16

he had explained them, were in his eyes simply lacking in intelligence. To him harmony was the natural state of affairs which would be achieved if proper intellectual processes were followed, and the notion that there could be more than one viable view about any issue worth considering was foreign to his character.

Otto was fighting a defensive battle. Traditional Treasury scrutiny of detailed estimates submitted by well-informed and amply staffed departments could not, he saw, stem the rising tide of public expenditure, especially when Reggie Maudling was Chancellor and Edward Boyle Financial Secretary. In a battle over any particular item, or indeed over a proposal for an overall cut, the expenditure department was likely to win. So the expenditure departments themselves must be driven to modify their demands by prearranged and enforceable limits on their programmes over a period of years. Hence the Public Expenditure Survey, still in current use, which he was at that time installing.

The quinquennial system for financing the universities had some resemblance to what Otto was proposing to apply for all the spending departments. Once the university money was settled it was supposed to be settled, and so was at least a fixed commitment. The counterpart in the bargain was freedom of action by the UGC and the universities in distributing the grant. But in practice it was not so simple. One reason was that in the new Public Expenditure Survey system the roles of Treasury and expenditure departments were meant to be clear and distinct – umpire and postulants. The already sizeable commitment for universities had to be brought to the Public Expenditure Survey by the Treasury itself. It was like the umpire going in to bat, and deducting his score from that of the other players.

The Treasury had already agreed to Keith Murray's massive programme of university expansion and encouragement. Between August 1957 and January 1960 the salaries of university staffs had been increased by a total of $28\frac{1}{2}$ per cent – much in excess of the then rate of inflation – and compensation had been paid by way of supplementary grant; the designation of seven new universities had been approved; capital programmes had been raised from £12m to a more or less guaranteed £15m a year (exclusive of fees, sites, furniture and equipment) for the four years starting in 1960. Most striking of all, the quinquennial settlement of 1957 had itself been reopened on a plea from the UGC that by its end the universities would have taken some 8,000 more students than the settlement had allowed for, so more funds were needed, 'otherwise the plans for the development of the universities on which the settlement was based could not but be vitiated'. The reason, though never I think publicly stated, was almost certainly a failure to foresee that annual increases of *intake* (corresponding to the rising number of suitable applicants) create a forward commitment at compound interest in terms of student places, because each student stays at the university for three or more years. Thus, if one works on the principle that the size of universities ought to be governed by the size of the annual age-groups in the population, the number of places required will increase more rapidly than the size of the age-groups when they are expanding, and will decline more slowly when they are contracting. Whatever the reason for the university 'overshoot' in 1957–62 it led to the first breach in the system of quinquennial settlements and the implicit bargain that underlay them. But it was a breach on the UGC side.

In 1959 the previous aim of a maximum of 135,000 students 'by the mid-sixties' had been raised to a maximum of 175,000 'by the late sixties or early seventies'; and in 1961 the capital programmes for the next two years, already put up to £15m each, were raised to £25m each, with promises of at least the same for 1964 and 1965. The first major computer programme (£2m over and above all other programmes) was agreed in the same year.

All this is faithfully reported in UGC's interim report on the years 1957 to 1961, which appeared while the Robbins Committee was in its early stages of deliberation.[1] It has gone unsung mainly because of the much larger and more spectacular proposals of the Robbins Committee, which many people think included the seven 'new' universities. I have even heard of them referred to as 'The Robbins universities'.[2] They should be called 'the Murray universities'.

Murray was subject to little check or competition within his own office, which then occupied a dignified house in Belgrave Square. The current Secretary, though in those days the equal of the Chairman in rank, wielded no influence. He was a former High Commissioner in Ceylon displaced by independence, named Sir Cecil Syers, who was celebrated for venturing nothing on a proposal except that he would consult his Chairman. His deputy and ultimate successor, E. R. Coples-

---

[1] *Interim Report of the University Grants Committee for the years 1957 to 1961*, Cmnd 1691, HMSO, presented April 1962.

[2] Sussex, York, Lancaster, Warwick, Essex, Kent and East Anglia. The Robbins Report did indeed recommend the founding of six more new universities in England, but none of these were ever established – see below.

The Treasury

ton, was a far more significant figure who contributed a dash of earthiness, even of cynicism, to Murray's unrelenting crusade. 'Cop' was immensely able and engaging but, unlike most people who become involved in educational issues, he was not closely engaged.

From one point of view all the Treasury had to do with the stream of advice it received from the UGC was to accept it. Indeed it had no sources of information on which to form a different judgment. Yet, as I very quickly found, the Treasury's formal responsibilities for the grant became anything but light at a time when public interest in the universities was rapidly gathering. Questions in Parliament about the universities, adjournment debates about them, had to be handled by Treasury Ministers. Parliamentary committees interested in one aspect or another of the universities demanded Treasury witnesses. As much of the resulting work as possible was, of course, shipped off at once to the UGC, but there can be no denying that part of my division, through sheer force of circumstances, was developing the characteristics of a miniature education department, though without access to the information and contacts such an organisation would normally have.

The massive growth of the universities, which the Treasury had already accepted but felt it was now unable to handle through the existing machinery, was the main reason for setting up the Robbins Committee, which was at its earliest formative stage when I arrived at the Treasury. This helps to explain the emphasis in the terms of reference on the need to review the *pattern* of higher education – and indeed the emphasis in the Report itself on institutions and the machinery of government. So far as *expansion* went, the Treasury felt that having been led by the hand by the UGC and having agreed to almost everything it asked, nothing very fearful need be expected. No direct invitation to consider further growth was extended in the terms of reference.[3]

Several other major matters already decided need to be fitted into the context of the Robbins Committee's creation. These lay in the field of the Education Departments – the Ministry of Education (for England and Wales) and the Scottish Education Department.

[3] 'To review the pattern of full-time higher education in Great Britain and in the light of national needs and resources to advise Her Majesty's Government on what principles its long-term development should be based. In particular, to advise, in the light of these principles, whether there should be any changes in that pattern, whether any new types of institution are desirable and whether any modifications should be made in the present arrangements for planning and coordinating the development of the various types of institution.' Treasury Minute, 8 February 1961.

19

Ever since the end of the War it had been a commonplace to say that the future of the country depended on the extension of technical education.[4] Much, much had been done about that in the universities. Of 268 building projects authorised by the UGC between 1957 and 1962[5] 91 were devoted to science, and of these 34 were for engineering and other technical subjects. The massive development of Imperial College had taken place outside, and as an extra to, the normal university programme. But apart from this – and the word 'apart' is designed to have emphasis – the vast and barely comprehensible network of local authority technical colleges had been propelled into reform by the Ministry of Education, and ten of the larger local colleges had been designated in 1957 as institutions supported by direct grant from the Ministry with the resounding title of colleges of advanced technology.[6] A national qualification equivalent to a degree – the Diploma in Technology – had been created to recognise their advanced courses, notably (the greatest innovation of the scheme) the 'sandwich' course, in which academic study and industrial experience under tutelage were mingled.

Otto had a curious notion – it was one of his few misconceptions – that the colleges of advanced technology (CATs) were cheaper than universities for the subjects they taught. In fact they were generously financed both in capital and recurrent terms. They began to develop research interests. Above all, since they were financed on an annual line-by-line basis in negotiation between their administrations and the Department, there was little internal pressure on them of the kind there was on universities to live within set limits.

Psychologically the CATs were very important because they arose out of the womb of the educational system as it had been fertilised since 1944. That system had always been kept at a distance from the universities. The CATs were consequently the pride and joy, the favoured children, of the Ministry of Education, which till recently had lain among the copses and fringes of Whitehall.

There were several features that set the Ministry of Education apart, and made it an odd member of the Whitehall family. Its founding statute of 1944 had given it a general responsibility for ensuring an

---

[4] I use this term to cover all higher and further education leading to a qualification in applied science – engineering in all its branches, together with chemistry and biology aligned to industrial purposes.

[5] See *University Development 1957–1962*, Cmnd 2267, HMSO, 1963, Appendix I.

[6] Aston, Bradford, Chelsea, Brunel, Salford, Bristol (later Bath), Cardiff (later UWIST), Loughborough, Northampton (Clerkenwell) (later City), and Battersea (later Surrey).

adequate system of education, but had conferred on it very few specific powers, and very little money under its immediate control. Its responsibilities were confined to England and (with certain inbuilt restrictions) Wales, for in Scotland there was a separate and proud education department as part of the powerful constellation constituted by the Scottish Office. Its traditional task of regulating educational standards through an inspectorate, once described as consisting of several hundred lieutenant-colonels, was carefully cocooned away from both its bureaucrats and its Ministers.

Thus its main relations were not with other Whitehall departments but with organised educational interests – local education authorities and their organisations (especially the latter), voluntary bodies, educational associations and educational trade unions. Its traditional concerns were not administration or control but structures and patterns, and it was only by manoeuvring these that it could hope to discharge its overall responsibilities. The grammar of Curzon Street was the difference between a voluntary aided school and a special agreement school, between a Director of Education and a Chief Education Officer, between an advanced course and a course of further education.

But along with this arid grammar went a far more interesting syntax. If the Ministry of Education had little administrative or direct financial power, it nevertheless had a clear duty to plan for the future, to foresee the incidence in the rise (and possibly the fall) in the demand for particular levels of education, and the sort of social and economic conditions for which education would have to operate. In this sense it was very much the heir of the post-war reconstruction and the Attlee years, during which most of its ablest officials had been recruited: and in the fifties it was very much a department of officials. Not all the officials approved of this tendency towards what might be called a fabian approach, but it nevertheless had great intellectual appeal in a department which was sedulously denied access to the substance of education.

For all these reasons the Treasury of the 1950s regarded the Ministry of Education with particular wariness. It had no real control over the greater part of the huge sums of public money[7] spent on education, so it could evade direct responsibility for all but a fraction of it. Its main administrative effort seemed to consist of brahminical exercises

---

[7] Much of it indeed rate-borne, but not the less public expenditure on that account in the eyes of the Treasury. But most of it flowed from the Exchequer through rate support grant and rate equalisation grant distributed by the Ministry of Housing and Local Government under statutory formulae.

which had neither a financial nor an educational effect of any moment. But at the same time it came forward with figures and forecasts which vibrated with financial consequences. The Treasury sought, therefore, to bring all the pressure it could on Curzon Street to install more effective financial controls, even if this meant bringing more of education within the ring-fence of central accountability. These pressures were applied with particular vigour to technological education – on which the Treasury were very willing to spend money provided they could see where it went – and to the building programme.

The planners of Curzon Street responded to these pressures. Its representatives were indeed the guardians of a system of indirect administration which depended on diplomacy rather than control; but they were not averse from adding to the educational system, even if it meant that their department had to shoulder direct responsibilities. Even at its more ingenious and adventurous moments the Ministry preserved its sober, homespun style. Nevertheless – and especially in the field of higher education – it began to develop the idea of a 'public sector' in which its own control would be more effectively exerted, and it was in this light that it fostered the CATs.

The third limb of the system of higher education was made up by the institutions for the training of teachers and this subject also lay at the centre of Curzon Street's planning. The origins of the teacher-training colleges (to give them their old name, still then current) lie in the very beginnings of the state education system, with its historic compromises on denominational education and the arrival of local authorities on the scene. There were more than 150 colleges (counting Scotland) and the great mass of them, in the 1950s, were modest, unpretentious institutions each numbering a few hundred students following a two-year course. In the late 1950s the pressing need for more teachers caused the colleges to be propelled into a great programme of expansion, reinforced by pressure from the profession (which triumphed in 1960) that they should offer a course of three years rather than two. Thus expansion had to be carried out at a 33⅓ per cent surcharge and the colleges became part of the 'pattern' of higher education the Robbins Committee was to be asked to review.

Nevertheless this part of the Robbins remit was to fit ill with the rest. Though grouped rather uneasily in Institutes of Education affiliated to universities, the colleges were rooted in the soil of local authority and voluntary body education. What was more their expansion (and, as was later to be found, their contraction) was geared not to any supposed or actual need for higher education as a whole, but to the prospective need for teachers as revealed by the birth rate, by proposals for expanding the size of the school system, by the ultimate objective of ROSLA,[8] and by pressure of the teachers' unions for smaller classes. While it is true that the colleges – especially when they began to provide a three-year course – provided places for many who could have found their way into the university system if there had been room for them, the principles shaping the size, nature and government of the system of teacher training could not be the same as those determining higher education as a whole. It had grown out of, and was determined by, the school system. And for that reason the intention was more or less to double the number of students in it within the decade.

But the most considerable reforms generated by the Education Departments during the years immediately before the appointment of the Robbins Committee concerned students and the support they received from public funds. *Grants to Students*, a report of a committee under Sir Colin Anderson appointed in 1958, was presented in May 1960.[9] It is now hardly remembered and little studied. It is not so much as referred to in the Robbins Report itself. Yet its recommendations, which were rapidly carried into law while the Robbins Committee was actually in session, are still the foundation of our system of student support.

It is obvious that the cost of higher education includes not only what is paid to sustain the institutions as such, but what is needed to sustain those who study in them: or at least so it appears at first sight, because, as I have already pointed out, history has determined that thinking about higher education in this country should be dominated by the concept of the 'full-time student', whose time should be entirely available to pursue study.

The Anderson Committee was brought into existence to tidy up the arrangements for supporting students that had grown up in the last fifty years. It was faced with the ancient system of awards made directly by institutions (mostly Oxford and Cambridge colleges and other charities); by the highly selective national competition on A-level

---

[8] Raising of the School Leaving Age to sixteen. This was provided for as a future development in the 1944 Act. The natural tendency to stay voluntarily beyond fifteen, the argument that those who wanted to leave on reaching that age would hardly profit by being forced to stay, and the expense, caused this ambition to be deferred for many years. Some enthusiasts wished to raise the age to eighteen.
[9] Cmnd 1051.

results known as state scholarships; and by local authority support (known in the trade as 'county scholarships') for those in their areas who gained places at universities. Over these last the local authorities exercised a certain degree of discretion, some authorities being more generous than others; but on the whole very few of those who had secured places at universities were refused support if they lacked other resources.

Finding as they did that something like 90 per cent of those who got places at universities in the small university system of 1958 qualified in one way or another for support, the Anderson Committee decided that the whole thing should be swept away in favour of a uniform national system of entitlement, subject perhaps (though on this they were divided) to a parental means test. Admission to this entitlement was conditional on ordinary residence in Britain, the achievement of two A-levels and acceptance by a university.[10]

This decision had immediate and long-term consequences of the most far-reaching character, none of which were fully foreseen.

Here we are talking not about the support of institutions to greater or lesser extents, or about the need of the country for qualified persons, or about structures, or about the spiritual value of a community of scholars, but about the creation and support of a class consisting of the most intelligent and energetic individuals just discovering their powers.[11]

The Anderson Committee gave definition to this new national class. Almost overnight the National Union of Students acquired a new, national role to negotiate on its behalf about the boundaries and extensions of the scheme; and in large measure had the support of the university administrations, who were necessarily interested in maintaining the charges they made to students for food and accommodation at adequate levels.

The Anderson Committee received no evidence from either the UGC or the Treasury about the probable expansion of the universities, though they were aware of intentions to raise full-time student numbers

[10] For some reason the colleges of advanced technology, though included in the scope of these 'mandatory' awards, were not included in the calculation of costs; nor were the teacher-training colleges, about which the Anderson Report is almost entirely silent despite the current proposals for their expansion.

[11] Part-time students of course include many such persons; but they did not benefit from any part of the mandatory awards recommended – not even towards their fees or books. 'We wish to stress that the award-making body should be generous in making grants towards the *educational* expenses of students studying part-time for high professional qualifications' was the furthest the Committee would go (paragraph 56).

to 135,000, or even more. Their costings – the highest of which were made on this figure – were therefore deceptively low in the light of events shortly to happen and made no allowance at all for help below degree level or its equivalent, or even for the 'generosity' with which they urged that the part-time degree student should be treated. Even so it was an increase of £10m a year if the parental contribution was retained – as it was. If the costing had been done on the figure of 170,000 full-time students which was already being discussed at the UGC, and to which capital programmes were aligned, the recommendations of the Anderson Committee would have come out at over £40m as against 1958–9 costs of £21m. And this omits postgraduates and teacher training. Their whole thinking was in terms of a small – a relatively small – higher education system, and with the much larger one which was just round the corner they, and everyone else, seemed unconcerned. It is odd to reflect on what would have happened if the question of reforming the student grant system had been considered by, or after, the Robbins Committee and not before it. As it was, that Committee was handed a virtual blank cheque for the support of additional student numbers; but then the Treasury was still hoping that the expansion it had already set in train would be thought sufficient, and that Robbins would do little more than solve the problems embodied in the word 'pattern' which had been embroidered so prominently into the terms of reference. The Anderson Committee said that everyone who could get into full-time higher education should have a grant. The Robbins Report completed the edifice by saying that everyone who wanted higher education and reached the required standard should have a place to go to.

The national system of mandatory grants was necessarily seen by the student world as akin to a wage, rather than as the social benefit which in fact it was. This accounts for the energy with which student organisations have always attacked the parental means test, which directly contravenes the wage concept.

Having distinguished the largest waves in the tide which ran so strongly in favour of higher education at that time, it is worth considering whence and how it generated such strength as to become a dominating political and social issue. The answer to this is usually given in demographic terms of the increased birth rate after the War ('the bulge') and the tendency to stay longer at school as a result of the 1944 extension of secondary education ('the trend'). These two quantifiable factors compounded each other and in turn persuaded the Education Departments, the UGC, the Treasury and the Robbins Committee of the urgent need to plan for an expansion of higher education. This was the more readily accepted because of the general agreement that a much larger number of highly educated people, above all in science and technology, was needed in the interest of prosperity and progress.

I have never felt that these arguments, intellectually powerful though they are, quite explain the strength of feeling which bore up the Robbins proposals and made the leaders of both parties place higher educational expansion in the forefront of their programmes.

One important source of it lay in the educational system itself, which since 1944 had developed an impetus of its own both in the numbers it employed and in the strength of its organisations. For both schools and teachers the number of pupils brought to a level which fitted them for higher education was an obvious measure of success; and it was therefore the teachers and the schools, as well as the pupils, who were frustrated and disappointed if places did not expand to match the numbers fit to fill them.

At the same time aspirations for the higher education of their children were shared by a far greater number of parents than ever before. Above all these were the parents to whom the War years, and their own energy and ability, had brought positions of responsibility and security which originally, in the absence of higher education, they had never expected to reach. These positions brought them into contact with, and often made them immediately subordinate to, graduates who had moved up the ladder far more rapidly than they had themselves.[12] Such people naturally saw a university education as a precious asset to their children. The motive power of the demand had, indeed, deep springs in social change and rising expectations.

[12] The expansion of the education service and the creation of the National Health Service created tens of thousands of middle-ranking posts for non-graduates. The civil service, which had enormously expanded during the War, provides an even more striking example, for even in 1960 it still preserved an Administrative (largely graduate) Class and an Executive (non-graduate) Class. Much the most rapid expansion had been in the Executive Class, and far more managerial work was being done by it at senior levels than before the War.

III

Picture of a Committee

An unexpected preliminary difficulty delayed the launching of the Robbins Committee in February 1961, and caused it to take a peculiar constitutional form. The original idea had been that it should take the form of a Royal Commission – the most prestigious of government-appointed inquiries. But it was found that this stirred uneasy feelings in the universities where a folk memory lingered about the Victorian Royal Commissions. They had done terrible things. Not only had they abolished celibacy: they had swept away whole swathes of fellowships and diverted the funds to support chairs in modern subjects; they had thrown many other fellowships and scholarships open to competition; they had interfered outrageously in the internal government of universities and colleges. On the other hand an inquiry into such an important question could hardly be conducted at the level of an ordinary departmental or even interdepartmental committee. So it was decided to make it a departmental committee appointed by the Treasury, but supra-departmental in that it was appointed by the First Lord of the Treasury, namely the Prime Minister. The arrangement is, I think, unique.[1]

One thing was clear to the Committee and everyone concerned with it from the outset: there would be action on the report. Whitehall and the Committee thus had a sense of common purpose, and the Committee a degree of confidence and determination it would not otherwise have possessed. It also made the leadership of the Committee feel that something very like the scale of expansion it proposed would in fact be adopted. But perhaps, equally, the sense of common cause with Whitehall made the Committee over-confident when it came to structural proposals.

It was the intention from the first that Lord Robbins should preside. He was then just reaching sixty, and at the height of his powers. When I first met him he impressed me as a bland silver lion, all mass and

---

[1] Sir Keith Murray, the Chairman of the UGC, who exercised much influence in the discussions leading up to the committee's appointment, and in its composition, was also against making it a Royal Commission, not so much for the reason I have given, as to guard against any possibility that it might (like some Royal Commissions) become a standing body, and thus endanger the position of the UGC.

whiteness. His huge frame was surmounted by an enormous face and a mane of silvery hair. Along with his gentle manner one sensed a giant paw from which a claw or two would sometimes make a carefully modulated appearance. I have never encountered anyone except Otto who was more confident that he was right. It was a friendly, comforting confidence, and disagreement was tolerated: but made no impression.

There was a certain simplicity of mind about Robbins, which dogged his great abilities and magnificent personality. He loved government, and thought he understood its ways, so he was easily captivated by forms and structures. He saw before him high principles and noble goals, and was liable to ignore or wave aside brutal or inconvenient realities. He saw, correctly, that a moment had come in the history of higher education at which mere endorsement of official advice would fall short of the occasion. He intended from the first that his report should mark a great advance.

In some important respects there were gaps in the sympathies and experience he brought to the task, though there were none in his application and determination to be just and liberal to all. He knew little about schools and their problems, still less about local education authorities or the realities of teacher training. He appreciated the social and economic importance of science and technology, but not the motivation of scientists. When such matters as these were discussed he treated them, indeed, as subjects for careful study and analysis in which the opinions of those more expert than he should carry weight: but when it came to questions of structure, of administrative doctrine, and above all of academic principles and the benefits conferred by the experience of higher education those at once found a real home in his warm, generous and liberal nature.

The new committee was staffed and provided for on the scale of a Royal Commission: that is to say it had an Assistant Secretary (not a Principal, the next rank below) as its Secretary, assisted by a Principal; and independent premises in Spring Gardens where it constituted a regular office. It was assigned a research and statistical staff of three, and ten other staff, making a total secretariat of fifteen. The Departments mainly concerned – Treasury and the Education Departments – appointed senior officials as 'assessors' who sat with the Committee and acted as liaison officers with their respective ministries. In addition, of course, each department in Whitehall marshalled and produced oral and written evidence.[2]

[2] The assessors were Sir Keith Murray from the UGC, Anthony (later Sir Anthony) Part from the Ministry of Education, Harry Donnelly from the Scottish Education Department,

Neither the Secretary of the Committee, Philip Ross, nor his assistant, Brian Gerrard, exercised much influence on the Report, though Ross was a clever, cheerful, rising man in the Treasury, and Gerrard one of the ablest Principals of his generation at the Ministry of Education. In different ways they were engulfed by the tide of events and what had seemed golden professional opportunity led to two professional and personal tragedies. Neither can be blamed: the atmosphere was too heady, the pace too hot.

The research team was headed by Claus Moser, seconded from the London School of Economics where he was at that time Reader in Social Statistics.[3] After the Chairman he exercised much the greatest influence over the shape and impact of the Report. He found a field where the statistics were primitive, timorous and amateurish, and made them clear and compelling. There are two poles in statistical work: one is professional and sophisticated, the other presentational and journalistic. The Moser team captured both approaches. The figures spread through the Report and its appendices are built into an edifice with a comprehensiveness and consistency that can rarely have been equalled, and support the major recommendation in a way it is impossible to dislodge. The text of Robbins supplies the brass and wind: Moser's figures the strings.

Apart from the Chairman there were eleven members of the Committee, one of whom (Sir Edward Herbert) died before the work was completed. He was a ship-builder and bank director of distinction, and an engineer by training who had been director-general of prefabricated building during the War. He was the oldest member of the Committee, and, in the pattern of such compositions, represented the employing side of industry. A younger industrialist with engineering qualifications would have been a great advantage to the Committee.

Two members were drawn from the world of school education: Dame Kitty Anderson, then headmistress of the North London Collegiate, and Anthony Chenevix-Trench who was headmaster of Bradfield when the Committee was appointed and became headmaster of Eton while it was in session. Dame Kitty was approaching the end of a dis-

and – in the latter phases of the Committee – myself, from the Treasury. Much of the evidence from the Ministry of Education was prepared by Richard Jameson and William Reid. That for the Treasury was put together by a team of three – myself, A. J. Phelps (later Deputy Chairman of the Customs and Excise, then serving in the Treasury) and Ralph Turvey (then a member of the staff of LSE seconded to the Treasury and ultimately Chief of the Bureau of Statistics in the ILO).

[3] Later Sir Claus Moser, Head of the Government Statistical Service, Chairman of the Covent Garden Opera, and Warden of Wadham College, Oxford.

tinguished career, and was still full of fire. Mr Chenevix-Trench was
much younger – only forty-four – and seemed on the brink of glory,
but his contributions were few. The Report's chapter on Higher Education and the Schools dwells almost entirely on the transition from school
to university, and hardly at all on the changes in the schools which
would be needed to sustain a massive enlargement of higher education
with an emphasis on science and technology. The product of the
schools as they were was at most taken for granted, and the emphasis
was on the disappointment of sixth-formers worthy of university
careers.

Two members represented the world of educational training and
administration – one a trainer of teachers, the other a power in local
authority educational administration. Both, especially the latter, carried
more weight in the Committee than the two teachers.

Lionel Elvin was at the time Director of the Institute of Education
at London University, and belonged heart and soul to the wave of
doctrine on which Labour had come to power in 1945. Lean, dark
and intense, he had started his career as a history don at Cambridge
and had been the Labour candidate for Cambridge University in 1935.
In 1944 he had become Principal of Ruskin, Oxford's adult education
college, and in 1946 a member of the University Grants Committee,
on which he served till 1950, when he became Director of the Department of Education of UNESCO in Paris. He had been much concerned
in the preliminary planning of UNESCO and in the Council for World
Citizenship, and even after he returned to London and the Institute
of Education, international collaboration through the spread of culture
remained central to his interests.

Elvin carried weight on the Committee as its idealist, but was, I
think, compliant beyond realism when it came to discussion of the
future of teacher training. This was not the case with H. C. Shearman,
whose feet were planted firmly on the ground of local authority education.

Mr Shearman was sixty-five when the Committee was appointed,
and Chairman of the Education Committee of the LCC, whence he
went on to be Chairman (simultaneously) of both ILEA and the GLC
while the Robbins Committee was still in session. He had stood unsuc-
cessfully as a Labour candidate for Parliament as long ago as 1922,
and spent many years as a tutor–organiser in the Workers' Educational
Association and the extra-mural department of the University of London. He carried heavy guns which he was not afraid to level at the

Chairman, and when it came to the point did not hesitate even at formal dissent – with important consequences. He was not usually argumentative or disputatious, but he saw clearly the ground on which he was bound to stand.

There were two members of the Committee of whom it could be said that they belonged to the silent minority. These were Sir David Anderson, Professor of Accounting and Business Methods at Edinburgh University, and R. B. Southall, whose career had been with British Petroleum in South Wales, where he was Vice-President of the University College of Swansea. Altogether, though industry had three seats on the Committee, its voice was little heard.

The other four members were drawn from the university world, though they reflected very different parts of it; so for what it is worth it could be said that counting the Chairman, Sir David Anderson and Lionel Elvin, academics just had a majority on the Committee. The aim certainly was to assemble a group ranging widely outside academic life, but the non-academics included fewer strong voices, and the academics all came from universities. By an oversight which turned out to be important, there was no member drawn from the world of the technical colleges.

James Drever, the first of the 'mainstream' university members, was at that time Professor of Psychology at Edinburgh, and in 1967 became Principal of the newly severed University of Dundee. He was a mild, likeable, earnest Scot whose steady university career had taken him first to Edinburgh, then to Newcastle, and then to Edinburgh again. His role as a representative of the social sciences was little needed in view of the Chairman's passionate interest in that area.

Helen Gardner, then a Fellow of St Hilda's College, Oxford, was the only member actually teaching at either Oxford or Cambridge, and the only representative of the arts subjects in a professional sense. She had also taught at Royal Holloway College, London, and has since, as Professor Dame Helen Gardner, become one of the most eminent scholars of her time in English literature. Just as the instincts of Mr Elvin and Mr Shearman on university matters could be described as 'low', so in ecclesiastical terms those of Dame Helen were 'high'. This in some ways made her a natural ally of the Chairman, but, given her independence of mind, this was not always the result – an instance being the Chairman's strongly held view that the Report should point a threatening finger at the 'metropolitan' universities of London, Oxford and Cambridge as in need of separate, possibly self-induced, inquiry. When such issues arose Robbins adroitly and blandly sought to isolate his opponent amid an otherwise silent flock.

The one seat assigned to science was filled by Sir Patrick Linstead. As Rector of Imperial College he held one of the most important posts in the world of science policy, and the college itself was the most striking recent example of British university development. Linstead brought scientific eminence and influence to the committee, along with direct experience of the problems of expansion. Nevertheless a second member from the scientific world – perhaps a mathematician or a physicist – would have been valuable.

Finally there was the Vice-Chancellor of Bristol University, Sir Philip Morris. It is difficult to find a greater contrast than that between Robbins, the Chairman, and Morris, the most potent member of his committee: one leonine, eloquent and affable, the other almost clerkly, precise, unobtrusive and hard as a diamond. On a first meeting Morris struck one as insignificant. He seemed below average height, his hair was plastered down, his style was demure. Yet he was probably the most powerful university man of that time, and had a power stretching far beyond the universities.

He had been one of the first to read Philosophy, Politics and Economics at Oxford, and had gone on, following a lead given in the mid-thirties,[4] to educational administration as an Assistant Education Officer in Kent. The War, and the rapid expansion of the forces, brought him to Whitehall as Director of Army Education, and he played a major part in realigning it towards general subjects, particularly current affairs: a factor which, though immeasurable, had a great influence on the outcome of the general election of 1945.

Morris became one of the great men of the Attlee years – British delegate to the founding conference of UNESCO, chairman of numerous bodies concerned with broadcasting, education and health, Vice-Chancellor of Bristol University. For many years, through the positions he occupied, he was probably the most powerful man in the West of England, and there was almost no aspect of its life in which he did not take an interest. From 1955 to 1958 he was Chairman of the Committee of Vice-Chancellors and Principals, and during Sir Keith Murray's earlier period of office was one of his closest advisers. He was at heart a unifier, above all in education, which he saw as moving

---

[4] See, for instance, *UGC Report 1929–35*: 'Whatever the practical difficulties may be, it seems to us peculiarly paradoxical that Local Authorities should not avail themselves more freely than they do of the product of the Universities' (p. 31).

inexorably towards a coordinated, if indirectly administered, publicly supported system. No member of the Committee, not even the Chairman himself, had more influence over the final emphasis of the Report: indeed it could almost be said he was its architect.

One of the strongest influences acting on the Committee was pressure, for which there was evidence on every side, of family ambition to send sons and daughters to university: a pressure which, as I have said created the favourable political climate the Report encountered. It corresponded to Philip Morris's deepest instincts and past achievements. The parents of children then at secondary schools were, in substance, the people who had fought the War and had been his own educational audience through service education. They themselves had been born in the twenties or earlier, when secondary education had been a privilege and ideas of social mobility and personal development through formal education had just begun to gain a hold on the imagination. For most of those parents the university had been a dream. For their children the dream should come true.

For the Robbins Committee to succeed it had to deliver a report with which the universities would cooperate, as well as one the Government would accept. Morris stood even closer to this delicate point of balance than either Robbins himself or the Chairman of the University Grants Committee. He was himself a convinced expansionist and firmly believed that the enlargement of higher and further educational opportunity was the path towards a civilised and prosperous society. He also had a high regard for the Whitehall establishment as it then was, and for the arrangements it had for financing the universities. But he knew that there were those in the universities – some of them Vice-Chancellors and many others in the departments and faculties – who would have reservations, perhaps on grounds of the upheaval expansion would cause, perhaps from fear of dilution, perhaps out of anxiety that large additional infusions of Government money would lead to an unhealthy interest by Government in university matters. It was Morris's particular concern, and his achievement, to ensure that the Report should contain the maximum of reassurance to the universities on all these points, and to maintain contact with the universities informally while the Report was being drafted.

To some extent, then, there was an inner, unofficial group within the Committee, consisting of the Chairman, Morris, Linstead and Murray. The main themes of the Report – expansion, autonomy and the generalisation of the university model – are theirs.

33

The Robbins Committee was not launched into a calm university sea. Between 1960 and 1962 severe strains developed between the Government and the universities, of a kind that had not been known before. They arose, like many which succeeded them, from efforts to bring public expenditure under control.

The quinquennial settlement for the universities which had been made in 1957 was due to expire in 1962 so its sequel had to be negotiated while the Robbins Committee was at work. The proceedings for this were opened for the last time in the traditional solemn manner, by a formal meeting between the universities, each represented by its Vice-Chancellor and its Chairman of Council, and the Treasury, whose team on this occasion was headed by Henry Brooke, the Chief Secretary. No room in the Treasury building was large enough for the assembly, so it was held at Middlesex Guildhall, and I have never seen so many men in black jackets and striped trousers in one place. Even in 1961 the costume was far from being a normal working uniform.

I do not think the British universities have been headed by a more distinguished group of Vice-Chancellors than at that time. They included not only Philip Morris, who was one of the principal spokesmen, and his brother Charles, the Vice-Chancellor of Leeds, but Sir Robert Aitken of Birmingham, Sir William Mansfield-Cooper of Manchester, Sir Malcolm Knox of St Andrews, and Sir Douglas Logan, the Principal of London University. After that meeting Otto remarked to me that Vice-Chancellors were now what Admirals had been before the war of 1914.

Every one of those I have mentioned had already achieved massive developments in his university, and had plans in readiness that were more massive still. Birmingham was sweeping up the hillside from the early redbrick Chamberlain rotunda; the plans for a campus more than a mile long at Manchester were already in preparation; large tracts of Bloomsbury had been earmarked for the new buildings that now surround the Senate House. A similar vision existed at Leeds.

The Vice-Chancellors of the great provincial universities saw the possibility of emancipation from the old metropolitan institutions and development towards the examples set by major state universities across the Atlantic; but they had noted the dependence of those great institutions on local politicians and industrialists, which was confirmed by their own experience of local government. Autonomy within a centrally financed national system was infinitely preferable. Diverse as these great men were in their origin and experience, they were supremely confident that they had to safeguard their institutions from any inroad by the central Government from which finance would come. Sir Robert Aitken of Birmingham, an impressive austere medical man from New Zealand, perhaps took the highest view of autonomy. But Sir William Mansfield-Cooper of Manchester was not far behind. He was a constitutional lawyer, energetic, affable and rotund, who had gained his original qualifications by part-time study and risen to national and international eminence on the university scene. Sir Douglas Logan, Principal of the University of London, then and for long afterwards towered in the university world. As the permanent Principal under Vice-Chancellors serving for only two years, he had unrivalled knowledge and continuous control of a machine which was in effect a subsidiary grants committee for the congeries of institutions which made up Britain's largest university.

The Treasury was put in a position of acute difficulty over the negotiations which followed. Having set up the UGC as a 'chosen instrument' for assessing the needs of the universities, it was in no position to dispute in detail the traditional but expensive submission that the UGC produced to justify the settlement proposed down to 1967. Nor was it easy for it to ask the UGC (as another department would have been asked) to go away and produce a cheaper solution. The only practicable tactic was the crude one of insisting on a lower figure, and refusing to accept any element which could be held to anticipate the results of the Robbins Report.

The battles on this issue were long and fierce – longer and fiercer perhaps because this was the first time the Treasury had seriously questioned the UGC's total bids, though of course under the conventions it was perfectly entitled to do so. Otto had discovered the word 'cost-effectiveness', which he ceaselessly hammered into Murray at the many difficult meetings they held at that time. The struggle over capital expenditure was particularly bitter, since even if it were conceded that in the immediate future the number of students would have to rise to maintain opportunity, the age-groups coming forward in the earlier seventies would be smaller again, and were unlikely to touch the 1965 figure until the middle eighties.[5] Surely, argued the Treasury, temporary pressure did not justify adding so much to the already large programme of permanent buildings, and if the plea was for enlargement

[5] See Robbins report (*Report of the Committee on Higher Education*, Cmnd 2154, HMSO, 1963), Table 25 (p. 56).

of opportunity, that could wait for Robbins and be spread over a number of years; for the time being that argument prevailed.

Relations between the Treasury and the UGC were subjected to further strain by the first chapter in the long and unhappy history of university salaries. Until then the arrangements had worked well enough, even though the formal structure hardly corresponded to the realities of the situation. Everyone knew that the money came from the Exchequer and that the scales required the approval of the Government; but in form each university, for sound institutional reasons, employed its own staff. Strictly speaking they were entitled to make their own bargains with each academic employee: in practice national rates allowing for a certain amount of flexibility (not very much) had long been accepted, and but for this it would have been impossible to estimate university costs, consisting as they do primarily of staff salaries.

This painful and complicated issue will arise again in this narrative. It is enough here to say (apart from observing that the subject has never gone right) that on this occasion Selwyn Lloyd, the Chancellor of the Exchequer, was concerned about the wages spiral of about 5 per cent and had declared the first of many incomes policies, 'the pay pause'.

Incomes policies must be simple if they are to be generally understood. They cannot therefore be sophisticated enough to take account of all the circumstances of real life. Whatever the device adopted, reasoned argument ceases with its adoption, for there can be no exceptions. In the case of Selwyn Lloyd's 'pay pause' all pay claims submitted after a certain day were placed in suspense and could not be proceeded with, whatever the case for them might be. The submission in respect of the university teachers arrived at the Treasury a day later than the appointed day, so, like the oath of Macdonald of Glencoe, it was ruled out of order.

The matter, like Macdonald's oath, was especially envenomed by an argument – the one ground for argument there could be – that the date on which the claim arrived at the Treasury was not the date on which the claim had been 'submitted'. Many months had elapsed since the university teachers had submitted their original claim to the university managements, and the document sent to the Treasury embodied the conclusion of the negotiations, blessed by the University Grants Committee, and sought no more than formal approval. On this issue the University Grants Committee came very near resignation.

During the first two years of the Robbins Committee's deliberations, therefore, relations between the Government and the Treasury on the one hand and the UGC and the universities on the other were very tense indeed; and during that time, quite naturally, public expectations about the new world of higher education that was going to emerge from the Report as part of 'the modernisation of Britain' were rising. Higher education occupied the centre of the political stage. Universities alone were the subject of eighty-three Parliamentary Questions in 1962 – an unprecedented number. Letters to the Chancellor and the Financial Secretary about university matters from members of the public and of Parliament came in shoals. At one point, bewildered by the massive artillery being brought to bear by the universities, Selwyn Lloyd called for a list of all the Chancellors of universities, most of whom he might expect to encounter unawares in the course of his social and ministerial life.

In the midst of this tension Harold Macmillan made the melodramatic reconstruction of his Government known popularly as 'the night of the long knives', which involved the departure from the Treasury not only of Selwyn Lloyd, the Chancellor, but of Henry Brooke, the Chief Secretary, and Sir Edward Boyle, the Financial Secretary, all of whom were necessarily identified with the 'pay pause'. Their successors (Reginald Maudling, John Boyd-Carpenter and Anthony Barber) set out on a policy of reconciling the universities with the Government. The salaries issue was cobbled up. The UGC was visited and addressed by the new Chief Secretary – a most unusual proceeding for the period; encouragement was given to the projectors of business schools on the transatlantic model; the development of the Robbins recommendations was followed by Ministers with the closest attention and it began to be abundantly clear that they were likely to accept a very large expansion indeed.

The Robbins Committee held its last meeting, and signed its Report on 23 September 1963. The Report was presented to Parliament and published in just over a month: but not by the Prime Minister who had commissioned it. On 23 October Mr Macmillan himself was succeeded by Sir Alec Douglas-Home.

IV

A Critique of the Report

The Robbins report of October 1963 appeared at a critical moment in the history of public opinion and is one of the great state papers of this century, and possibly the last of its line. Only the Beveridge Report of 1943 and the Poor Law Report of 1909 can compete with it for copiousness, cogency, coherence and historical influence. It contains memorable passages and is informed by a consistent intellectual attitude. It is extraordinary to think that the investigation on which it rested as well as the composition of the Report itself took less than two and a half years.[1]

What is more, it was produced under increasing pressure that it should be ready in time for the coming general election. There was nothing wrong in this at all. Higher education was a burning issue. No doubt advantage was hoped for by the Conservatives then in power, with their slogan 'Modernisation of Britain', but their opponents were no less committed and the general interest made it absolutely right that the Report should be before the country when it came to vote. Nevertheless, pressure of time caused the Committee to concentrate on certain issues it saw as essential and not to explore – or almost not to explore – their deeper and wider implications, as well as some special questions which caused trouble later on.

It hardly needs saying that the Report is dominated by two themes: the expansion of higher education to make it available to all those qualified to receive it and wishing to do so; and the autonomy of the institutions giving it, not only in themselves, but in the governmental and financial system through which they receive support.

I was not, and never have been, opposed to either of these theses. But it has never been demonstrated that they form the perfect combination for the achievement of each, nor does the Report do this.[2] The

---

[1] The Committee held 111 meetings, heard 121 witnesses formally, received 412 written memoranda, made 7 visits abroad, carried out several statistical surveys, and cost £128,770. It often met over the weekend.

[2] The Committee examined a number of foreign models, and visited the Soviet Union, the United States, France, Germany, the Netherlands, Sweden and Switzerland. 'In our travels abroad', it said at paragraph 709, 'we have seen much that is admirable and much from which this country might well learn. But in this respect [i.e. the relationship between

two are, in fact, closely, though not perhaps obviously, connected by the concept of 'qualified' in the first of the theses, which relates not merely to a standard achieved in public examinations but to acceptance by an institution acting autonomously.

The weaknesses of the Report lie not in its proposals but in its omissions. Some of these could be perceived at the time, others only by hindsight. It is fair to say that this criticism extends also to certain of the decisions taken immediately after the Report, which ignored future problems to which the Report did draw attention.

Perhaps the biggest inadequacies come from over-optimism about the wider consequences of expanding the system quickly and by an order of magnitude. 'We think that any institution is under an obligation so to organise itself that neither teachers nor students feel themselves mere parts of an impersonal machine. There is a range of problems here that has not yet been fully investigated.'[3] But apart from the heavy hints that Oxford, Cambridge and London stood in need of administrative reform, the problems of managing large institutions with thousands of employees and tens of thousands of students received little attention. The existing redbrick pattern of court, council, senate and Vice-Chancellor dividing authority between them was confidently recommended.

So was staffing on the basis that every teacher would also be engaged in research. It is undoubtedly true that achievement in research gives authority to the teacher by convincing the pupil that in imparting the syllabus the teacher speaks not only from a greater depth of knowledge but from work at the frontier and commitment to the subject. What is more, the divorce of research from teaching, which is common in countries outside the British tradition and a matter of policy in communist states, not only impoverishes teaching but gives the state too great a purchase over the direction of research. Although the Committee devoted much space in its Report to this question, and conducted a survey of the time spent by university teachers on different aspects of their work, it flinched from examining the consequences for research which would flow from the expansion of student numbers which they proposed. If staffing is on the basis that every teacher has time for research, it does not follow that the increased amount of research implied is in itself desirable, or indeed will be done at all. Still less

the state and institutions] we have seen nothing that has induced envy of the position of other systems and much that has led us to prefer the British.'

[3] Paragraph 472.

can it be assumed that the research time attributable to expansion of student numbers will be in the areas where research effort is most needed. In effect, therefore, the doctrine is liable to expand research in the subjects which attract most students, and starve it in those which attract few. It also, if pursued to its logical conclusion, means running down research (however valuable) if the number of students for any reason, either as a whole or in particular subjects, declines. There is also the question whether the time provided for research is so used. If the numbers concerned are small this does not matter, and the time can often be absorbed in other useful university work; but if numbers are large, it can lead to scepticism about professional commitment.

A second criticism of the Report as a whole is a deficiency of historical perspective. Its opening chapter describes the successively widening horizons of educational opportunity from the institution of compulsory primary education onwards, and draws the inference that growth in higher and postgraduate education logically follows. But apart from that the Report is a notably free-standing document, and ignores the cumulative effect of its recommendations piled on what had happened in the recent past. It is like watching a man leap across a crevasse. How could he have been but now on one side, and at this moment on the other?

The question of student support provides a striking example. As we have seen, the Anderson Committee on student grants, a few years earlier, had regarded its task more or less as a tidying-up operation. In a small university world which it was still a privilege to enter, a consistent system of state support for students, such as the Anderson Committee proposed, was rational and inexpensive. The evidence before them gave no hint that an enormous and rapid expansion in the number of students would soon become a matter of policy. While conceding that 'it is important that the student body should not be drawn from too narrow a field,' the Anderson Committee had gone on to calm doubts about expense by saying, 'We do not think it is likely that students will lightly move to far distant institutions; those who would benefit more from attending a local institution will still wish to do so.' The Robbins Committee regarded its expanded system as national in the sense that every institution would recruit throughout the country, and saw positive virtue in students living away from home. Two-thirds of the additional students would have to be provided with university residence. Departure from home was not only desirable to achieve an economic fit: it was an educational benefit.

A Critique of the Report

No separate chapter was devoted by the Robbins Committee to student support or to the effects of bringing large numbers of energetic and intelligent young people together far from home in purpose-built residence. Like the Anderson Committee, the Robbins Committee considered loans for student support, and, like the Anderson Committee, rejected them.

Certainly the Report tried to emphasise the idea that higher education would still be a privilege; but the whole gravamen – increasing numbers based on proportions of age-groups supported out of the mandated awards introduced by Anderson – made the plea sound hollow. Neither part-time students nor bright, poor children wanting to stay at school after sixteen received similar consideration to that given to a full-time student, who, once admitted, would be provided for.

There was a second respect in which the seemingly modest proposals of the Anderson Committee for a national system of student awards was dynamised in an unexpected way by the thinking of the Robbins Committee – though in this instance the effects were delayed. The increasingly trivial fees charged by universities had for many years past been treated as a charge on the student awards, and by the early sixties had come to constitute a derisory part of university income; so the Anderson Committee saw no difficulty in including the modest sum needed for fees in the bill for awards which was now to be met from central, not local, funds. It is far from clear that when the Robbins Committee recommended a substantial increase in the income derived from fees (a proposal which was not pursued until some time afterwards) it was in effect suggesting that most of the cost would come from any source but the Exchequer, just like UGC grant, though accounted for in a different way.

It may be too much to assert that the Robbins Report described a national system of higher education, but such was certainly its unspoken assumption and its aim. Each of the institutions – or at any rate those on which the Committee placed most value, the universities – wherever located, was thought of as having a national constituency and should in principle have parity of esteem with all the others. Nobody really believed this was or would be so, but the alternative of conceding the possibility of competition or variation was so invidious that it could not be thought of. Few, if any, other major countries have attempted such a noble feat. In the United States higher education, as they say, 'ranges all the way from the Ivy League to Podunk College'; Japan offers a jungle of public and private institutions; in Germany and Swit-

41

zerland the universities are organised by provincial or cantonal governments; even in France nobody would claim parity of esteem was evenly spread. The Robbins Report has as one of its most important principles a university world in which both competition and variation in attractive power are in principle eliminated. 'We believe any such disparity between the incomes and prospects of persons doing similar work in different universities, which are all in receipt of public funds, to be unjust; and we consider its effects to be harmful.'[4] In particular the magnetic influence of Oxford and Cambridge should if possible be reduced. So also with students. The system of support (including the provision of residence) should be such as to spread the choice of students to all parts of the system. Naturally a large cost went together with this.

The degree of expansion required, being based on the size of age-groups already in existence and due to reach the age of eighteen in successive years, was incontrovertible once the premise that opportunity should be at least maintained had been accepted. It is very important to remember that 'maintenance of opportunity' in the Robbins context did not mean that the size of the age-groups was the only determining factor. It meant maintenance of opportunity for those expected to reach qualifying level and seeking entrance, and was thus an academic as much as a social concept. This is particularly important if one bears in mind that the Robbins Committee expected a much more rapid growth in women entrants than in men, because more women, proportionately and absolutely, were going to qualify. It was necessary to make assumptions about the proportion of each age-group that would gain the minimum qualifications and aspire to higher education. Since these assumptions were cautious, the path proposed could only be disputed by those who were prepared to argue that the opportunities for higher education should decline, or that some aspirants should be put off with second best, or that the system as a whole should be watered down.

The scale – or rather the scales – of expansion recommended by the Committee caught the public imagination and ensured the Report's immediate success. I give the detailed figures in Appendix I (pp. 169–72). Put briefly, the Report set two specific targets in terms of full-time student numbers, one for 1967 (only four academic years ahead at the time of the Report was published), and the other for

[4] Paragraph 542.

42

1980. By the first of these dates the number of students in the higher education system as a whole (universities, further education colleges and teacher training) was to grow by 50 per cent; and by 1980 it was to grow by two and a half times the 1962 figure. In absolute numbers this meant adding 112,000 full-time students by 1967 and 342,000 by 1980, in which year the total was to be 558,000, compared with 216,000 in 1962. In this expansion the universities were to take a gradually increasing proportion of the new places required.[5]

The Committee did not attempt to apportion these large increases between men and women students. The evidence before it showed that although the number of women entering higher education was considerably lower than the number of men, it had been rising steadily for the past ten years, and was likely to go on doing so. The combined average rate of entry for both sexes as established up to 1962 was therefore taken as the starting-point in translating the age-groups into projected entries, which indeed implied an increase in the proportion of women students, as well as an increase in their numbers. In practice it is reasonable to say that the Committee envisaged a more or less equal ultimate distribution between the sexes of the extra places they proposed.[6]

The call to maintain opportunity, backed up as it was by irrefragable statistics, was the main social and political appeal of the Report; but it would not have found such overwhelming support if it had not been mingled and reinforced with a very different argument – the need, in a modern Britain, for much greater numbers of scientists and technologists. While this argument was also beyond dispute, it was quite separate from the demographic argument, and had different implications. The need for more scientists and technologists would have been true even if the demographic data had shown a decline in the numbers likely to seek university entrance; and the prospect of massive expansion in history, literature and social science, however civilised the picture it conjured up, would not by itself have been persuasive as a call on massive public funds.

This required the Committee to say something about the distribution of subjects of study within the expanded system it proposed. It did

---

[5] See Table 59 of the Report for the 1967 figures, and Table 44 for the 1980 figures. For the 'actual' 1962 figures there is a slight variation between two Tables, with Table 59 giving 3,000 more (219,000) than Table 44, which I have followed. The figures are set out in more detail, and compared with what actually happened, in Appendix I of this book.

[6] See Robbins Report, Appendix I, Section 7, Tables 33 and 34.

A Critique of the Report

this in very general terms, but emphasised the claims of science and technology, especially the latter, to a major share of the new places in contemplation. The Committee was aware that in the UGC's shorter planning horizon it was assigning two-thirds of the expansion already approved to science and technology.[7] For the longer term, down to 1980, the Committee proposed that arts and social science should be restrained to their existing proportion (though of course numbers would grow absolutely) and that the proportion studying medical subjects should actually decline. This left room for a large absolute increase in science and technology – 74,000 new places in 1967, and 174,000 by 1980. Well over half of these were to be in universities.[8]

The superimposition of this pattern of studies on the earlier principle of maintaining opportunity by reference to data which were primarily demographic and social had important consequences and surprising implications. Thus, if the 'extra places' in science and technology were equally divided between men and women, the number of women studying that group of subjects at universities would amost have to treble in five years, from about 12,000 to over 30,000; and increase more than eightfold to 99,000 in less than twenty years. The corresponding male students, on the other hand, would increase by less than half in the short term, and not much more than double in the longer term.[9]

Such a change, however just and desirable, implied a dramatic alteration in the pattern of studies in schools, in the attitude of the outlook of girls already at school, the attitudes of their families, and the habits of both sides of industry. The Report bears no stamp of awareness of these problems, and the time it would take to solve them if expansion on this pattern was to be accomplished. Indeed it left the balance of studies in teacher-training colleges – where the balance of school studies could be most directly influenced – completely unchanged even in the longer term.[10]

While it may seem improbable that student numbers would follow

[7] *UGC Interim Report 1957–61*, paragraph 11. The proposal was based on indications that the demand for science places was already growing, though it should be noted that Table V of the same Report showed that the increase of student numbers due to applications in science and technology between 1956 and 1961 was still well short of two-thirds: in fact 56 per cent.
[8] Robbins Report, Table 46 (p. 166), and Appendix I to the Report, Table 54 (p. 170).
[9] See Appendix II for more detailed figures.
[10] 'In Colleges of Education we do not think there are sufficiently firm grounds for assuming any change in the balance of studies' (Report, p. 165); 'In teacher training, the same balance between subjects has been assumed for 1980–81 as in 1962–63' (Report, Appendix I, p. 170).

the course I have just described, or even approximate to it, the consequences of their not doing so were bound to be very untoward. On the one hand the new science and technology places (i.e. the newly built science buildings and the increased number of qualified staff) would either not be used to their full capacity, or would not be filled by domestic candidates of the quality hoped for. On the other hand, whatever combination of these circumstances occurred, there would be increasing pressure – mainly from girls – to enter the arts, social science and medical faculties whose relative growth the plan restrained. If, to take an example, the schools provided four times as many admissible women science candidates by 1977 as they had done in the early sixties, there would in theory still be some 40,000 qualified girls seeking to enter arts, social science and medicine for which places were not provided under the plan; and about a similar number of places in science and technology would be filled either by male candidates of lower calibre than in the 1960s, or by students from abroad, or would not be filled at all.[11]

All this has been set out in some detail because it constituted a main deficiency of the Report and was responsible for many of the stresses which soon became apparent. It arose from the best of motives, and a wish to reconcile several different aims, all of them liberal: enlargement of opportunity, especially for women; multiplication of scientific manpower in the service of future prosperity; and a system of autonomous institutions that would nevertheless operate on a collective national plan. But the scale of distortion was very large indeed given the scale of the plan itself. The 136,000 additional university places in science and technology were the equivalent of at least a dozen universities the size of Oxford at the time.

Nor would the effect of such a distortion be confined to the universities. It would be felt in the remainder of higher education – the colleges of education and the further education colleges. To the extent that entry into university science and technology became easier, for the reasons that have been indicated, those colleges (which were also to be expanded) would find themselves short of science applicants.

---

[11] There is, I agree, one other possibility that in theory could have modified these consequences: namely that a larger proportion of the ablest male school-leavers would turn to science. Even this, however, would have taken time to happen; and the switch would have had to be very large indeed. In 1962 some 60 per cent of all men going to universities were entering faculties of science and technology. If this proportion had been raised to 80 per cent by the later seventies there would still have been some 50,000 science and technology places for women implied in the plan – a fourfold increase on 1962.

Throughout the system competition for science students would develop between institutions, with the least attractive institutions finding it difficult if not impossible to maintain standards of entry, and being driven to seek survival in other ways.

The Robbins Committee found as a historical fact that about 10 per cent of the student body in universities came from abroad, and in the absence of any other clear evidence of future demand it built that percentage into its estimates of places required. It can reasonably be said – and was indeed said in the Report – that there is no logical connexion between an expansion programme linked to British demography and educational attainment on the one hand, and the various powerful arguments for including students from abroad on the other. These arguments might indeed point to a greater commitment towards overseas students than British age-groups justified. They certainly would not support a decline in the numbers from overseas if, for a time, British age-groups shrank.

But the Report did not leave the question at that point. It drew attention to the large and indiscriminate subsidy received by foreign students under the existing arrangements, and recommended ways of bringing it under control by deriving more revenue from fee income and creating a fund from which the neediest students and overseas countries should be helped in accordance with policy on overseas aid.[12]

This part of the Robbins Report had very little notice, and seems largely to have been forgotten in the furious controversy on the subject of overseas fees which later arose. It must be seen in the context of the Committee's wish to see universities draw a much larger part of their income from fees – 'we recommend that the level of fees be revised so that in future they meet at least 20 per cent of current institutional expenditure. Some of us would prefer to see the proportion greater.'[13] While the Committee had other reasons for this recommendation, its bearing on the subsidy to foreign students played an important part.

However, the question of overseas students was left to fester, partly

---

[12] Paragraphs 174, 175 and 655. 'The total annual subsidy involved amounts at the present time to something like £9m.... It is however, an open question whether the aid is best given by subsidising fees.... But ... it involves a substantial subsidy over which the nation has no control and for which it receives no credit. Some students who come do not need a subsidy – they are the children of very rich parents – and few, if any, students realise they are getting one. We cannot think this is desirable. We do not suggest that a higher fee should be charged to overseas than to other students, but we recommend that the principles on which fees for overseas students are calculated ... should in future be uniform.'

[13] Paragraph 654.

because it was tied to the proposal for raising fees all round, which neither the universities, the UGC, the local authorities nor the Government wanted.

Whitehall must also share with the Robbins Committee the blame for another weakness in the Report: the absence of any serious discussion of medical education, which then absorbed roughly a quarter of all university expenditure, and does so still.

Medical education was not excluded from the Committee's terms of reference, and in view of its importance, both financially and in other ways, it may seem astonishing that in such a sweeping survey one can find only passing mentions of the subject. Medicine is ancient, yet socially relevant. One would expect it to occupy a central place in any picture of a university where it is taught, since it is concerned with applying science to humanity. Yet the tendency in universities is to tip-toe round the medical component, quietly lamenting the large share of university resources it gets, but otherwise leaving it severely alone. The Robbins Comittee did this.

They were encouraged to do so. No medical member was included in the Committee, and this was deliberate. In the traditional official thinking of both the Government agencies and the profession, the size of medical schools is governed by the need for doctors of the National Health Service, a concept often treated as capable of numerical definition but in fact just as elastic as any other in 'manpower planning'. This brings in political, social and financial questions which have little directly to do with education and can be of the most sensitive and alarming kind. It happened that just before my arrival at the Treasury a Committee under the chairmanship of H. U. Willink had reported on the needs for medical manpower, and to the delight of the Treasury had concluded that no expansion was necessary. Indeed there seemed to be a danger that there would be too many doctors. It is true that the statistical basis for this finding (much influenced by the British Medical Association, which was then in a restrictionist phase) was shot to pieces a few months after it was published, but that was too late. Instead, while the Robbins Committee was in session in 1962, the Treasury, on the proposal of the Health Departments, agreed to a 10 per cent increase in medical student numbers, without referring it to Robbins at all.

It would have been difficult for the Robbins Committee to deal fully with medical education as well as all the other questions it had to consider, especially within the time-span allotted to its work. But by

47

excluding it, and by allowing itself to assume that virtually no growth in medical education would be required, an important financial constraint which otherwise should have been present in its deliberations was removed. If the opportunity for studying medicine had been conceded by the Report to those 'qualified and willing' to undertake it in the same measure as it was in other subjects, the cost estimates would have been much higher. As it was, the 25 per cent expansion allowed for medical subjects down to 1981 grossly underestimated both student demand and any probable prediction for the needs of the Health Service. The job had to be done in the end by a separate Royal Commission under Lord Todd, and the chance of fitting this important subject into the general context of university growth was lost. The cost of the increase recommended by the Todd Commission, along with far-reaching structural reforms, either had to be added on to the existing commitment or could not be found at all.

I have referred at the beginning of this critique to a failure in the Report, at important points, to explore practical implications of what was proposed if they were likely to cloud an important theme, such as the autonomy of institutions and the need to maintain opportunity. The following are further examples.

The exemption of the universities from parliamentary audit could just about be defended when there were twenty-one institutions, most of them long established, but it was already under attack. Was it conceivable that it would still be acceptable for more than fifty university institutions, plus the teacher-training system, plus an unspecified number of promoted regional technical colleges at a projected cost of £742m a year of public money? The claim that the exemption originated in a recognition of the special needs of universities was difficult to sustain, for, as we have seen, it had been necessary only when, after the War, public funds began to make up more than half the income of universities.

The discussion of university staffing provides another instance. The Committee foresaw that in the period of rapid expansion in the immediate future which they called for 'there will be considerable difficulty in finding enough suitably qualified teachers', and urged that 'any inroads on present standards must be transitory, and redressed as soon as possible'.[14]

But how soon would that be? The Committee had no difficulty in

---

[14] Paragraph 819.

demonstrating that in the longer term any expanding university system will produce enough potential university teachers to staff itself, provided the rate of expansion is reasonably steady; but it was not the Committee's intention that the rate should be steady. It was fundamentally tied to demography, and in particular to a very rapid expansion in the years immediately ahead.

The Committee did indeed throw out some suggestions for easing the position in the immediate future: the retention of staff beyond retirement age; the employment of postgraduates for some duties; the recruitment of part-time teachers; improved technical and secretarial assistance to academic staff; and even 'extraordinary burdens on teachers in the way of additional duties and strain' – a course contradicted elsewhere in the Report[15] by the clear recommendation that staffing ratios should not be allowed to deteriorate.

Nowhere in the Report was it suggested that recruitment to a full-time academic post should be otherwise than for life. Tenure, indeed, was not discussed at all, but the absence from the catalogue of suggestions of any hint that full-time staff should be employed on a temporary basis during the short-term emergency implied that the tradition of tenure seemed so clear to the Committee that it hardly needed mentioning.

The Committee's calculations were that nearly a fifth of the graduates of 1960 (the actual figure is 18.4 per cent) would be needed to staff their immediate programme. Given tenure most of them would still be in office at the end of the century. By the early seventies the fraction needed (admittedly out of a much larger graduation) would be 10 per cent. Two consequences followed. There would be an appreciable margin of staff recruited at a lower standard occupying posts for the next forty years; and long before that it would become more difficult than it had ever been for the most brilliant graduates to obtain posts. The failure of the Committee, in its anxiety to demonstrate that staffing was practicable, to face the consequences by a serious discussion of terms of service had grievous results for the next generation.

One final instance should be added, for it perhaps caused more difficulty than any other problem flowing from the Robbins Report. The university model they knew and understood exercised so strong an influence on the Chairman and the majority of the Committee that they had little sympathy or understanding for any other. The teacher-

---

[15] Paragraph 532.

training colleges, the regional colleges, the colleges of advanced technology, even the Scottish universities burdened by the Universities (Scotland) Act 1889 and the powers it conferred on the Secretary of State
in that ancient and centralised kingdom, seemed so many maidens
in distress who, provided their work was well done, should be conducted into the haven of autonomy. The purposes of local authority
institutions, their links with local (or denominational) power and affection, the need to replace their work below degree level if they vanished
into the university world, the fact that their staff were not paid the
same as university teachers, were not discussed.

I am sure the Committee was right in its devotion to autonomy,
though it should not be regarded as a status peculiar to universities.
It encourages freedom of thought and initiative, makes for economical
administration, conserves standards and takes academic controversy
out of the political world by putting it where it belongs, in senates
and other university bodies. It means that university teachers are judged
by their colleagues, not by officials, that decisions on admission, promotion, appointment and distribution of work are taken within the proper
terms of reference, and that patronage and influence do not intrude
– at least intrude less than they otherwise would.

But, as we shall see, the Committee (or rather all but one of its
members) seriously underestimated the practical obstacles in the way of
of its ideal, and indeed added to them by treating the word 'university'
as almost equivalent to the autonomy which it considered to be so
important. It thereby, quite unconsciously, introduced an issue of
'status', with all its attendant jealousies, aspirations and protectiveness,
into a practical question of organisation which was already difficult
enough. A more evolutionary approach would have been more likely
to achieve its objective.

Thus the Report left many raw and ragged edges to those who had
to administer its consequences in Government and in the universities.
To the universities it left an admonitory and characteristic message
which bears the stamp of Morris rather than Robbins:

Clearly an institution must be free, if it is to maintain standards, to relate the
numbers it admits to resources that it has available. But if funds are available,
refusal to cooperate in national policies or to meet national emergencies is an unsympathetic attitude, and it would be easy to think of reasons why it should be overruled. On balance we are clear that it is in the long-run interest of all that such
an attitude should be tolerated. If, when all the reasons for change have been
explained, the institution still prefers not to cooperate it is better that it should

be allowed to follow its own path. This being so, it must not complain if various benefits going to cooperating institutions do not come its way.[16]

Cooperation was forthcoming. The rough edges were left behind.

The Report caught the mood of the time. It was right in many of its perceptions. Its case for a large and rapid increase in higher education on demographic, economic and social grounds was undeniable. In the face of it 'More means worse' was a hopeless, backward-looking slogan. The fear, expressed by some critics, that as graduates grew commoner their status (and the differential in income graduates had often secured) would be diminished, was correct but irrelevant. 'Many of them will finish up as bank clerks,' Otto remarked when we were discussing the Report, 'and why not graduate bank clerks?' The emphasis on science and technology was also justified, though its scale did carry a danger that more, in this case, might mean worse. The rhetoric in support of autonomy, apart from all its other advantages, favoured efficiency. Where, in broad terms, the Report failed, was in not appreciating that the scale and importance of what they were proposing could not in the end continue to be treated wholly as a kind of *Patrimonium Petri* if it was to be supported from public funds; and in not perceiving that the wider base of school and family would have to change just as much as the edifice Robbins proposed to build upon it, if the mansion was to be prosperous and happy.

[16] Paragraph 715.

V

The Great Plastic Period

The appearance of the Report and the White Paper in October 1963 opens the great plastic period[1] in higher education, which lasted until the enunciation of 'Binarism' by Anthony Crosland in his speech at Woolwich in April 1965. The public mood was one in which great numbers of things which in a normal period would take years to settle, if they could be settled at all, could be decided for good or ill in almost no time. The press, the public, the political parties, were full of enthusiasm for higher education, especially university education. Money flowed in abundance. The few voices that were raised in opposition and restraint were shouted down and muffled. Vast reorganisations in Whitehall took place. 'Lumps of raw flesh', Sir Maurice Dean[2] observed, 'are being hurled about.'

The general election of October 1964, which brought Labour into power under Mr Wilson, divides the period, and was in effect a boost rather than an interruption to existing policy in higher education. But since neither party was willing on this question to concede the running to the other, several of the most important decisions were taken in the last ten months of Conservative rule, the most important of these being the whole-hearted acceptance of the expansion proposed down to 1967, and assurances of good-will for the aims in the further future.

Almost equally significant decisions concerned the pattern of higher education – the issue on which the Robbins Committee had been set up to advise – and especially the arrangements in Whitehall. The Report had devoted many paragraphs to this, but the solution favoured by the majority was not adopted. It had been criticised effectively in a dissenting note by one member, H. C. Shearman.

The main body of the Committee suggested a 'Ministry of Arts and Science' coupled to an overarching Higher Education Grants Commission which, on the principles of the existing University Grants Commit-

---

[1] 'We must, in judging the most powerful of minds, take into account the influences to which they were exposed in the plastic period; and where imagination is visbly the predominant faculty, allowance must be made very largely indeed.' J. G. Lockhart, *Memoirs of Sir Walter Scott*, Macmillan, 1900, vol. iv. p. 328.
[2] See note 7 below.

tee, would finance all the institutions considered worthy of autonomous status, now or in future: universities, the colleges of advanced technology, the teacher-training colleges, such further education institutions as made the grade, the Royal College of Art and the College of Aeronautics. This noble department would also be responsible for museums and galleries, scientific research and the Arts Council. It would, in fact, be the Ministry for the Intelligentsia. Most of its finance would be settled through advisory committees and be outside the scope of audit by the Comptroller and Auditor General. The existing Education Departments in England and Scotland would be left with school education and as much of further education as was not judged worthy of autonomy.

There were two objections to this idea. One was that when it was examined it was a recipe for minimal change. It got rid of the anomaly by which the Chancellor of the Exchequer was saddled with extensive responsibilities over which he had no control, but only by putting another dummy in his place.[3]

The other objection was urged in Mr Shearman's note of dissent. The educational system would be subjected to dangerous surgery. He fastened particularly on the proposal to sever teacher training from the Education Departments. 'The Colleges of Education,' he said, 'will have no immediate administrative contact with those who have major responsibility, central and local, for the schools.' Worse still, a ladder would be raised up which institutions nurtured to success by the local education authorities and the Inspectorate of Schools would vanish, while those who remained at the bottom would complain and rebel.

The 'seamless robe' question, as it came to be called, was the one that started in my mind an analogy which can be applied over and over again to higher educational controversies: 'high church' and 'low church'. On the seamless robe of education the Robbins position is 'high church'. It stresses autonomy, faith in the capacity of the institution as such to see the light, along with a certain charm and elevation of style which implies a degree of detachment. Contrasted with this is the position founded on the belief that education should serve social ends and hence (on the congregational principle) should be accountable.

---

[3] Paragraph 784 of the Report gently suggests the powerlessness of the proposed Department: 'Since so much of the work will be done through grants committees, the whole would tend to be informed by a special degree of detachment and respect for the autonomy of the institutions and individuals ultimately concerned.' The Treasury was still, at that point, directly responsible for financing the Arts Council and most of the national museums and galleries, as well as the universities.

One is prelatical, the other evangelical. One emphasises the church and its necessary privileges; the other the text, its mission and its consequences. Of course there is an infinity of positions between the two, and most people are latitudinarians, but just the same the analogy not only helped me with eighteenth-century history but enabled me to place many other contributions to university disputes as tending to be either 'high' or 'low'.

The Whitehall aspect of the seamless robe controversy was settled by Sir Laurence (later Lord) Helsby, who was then Head of the Civil Service. The solution – the Department of Education and Science – was in substance 'low', but contained a concession to the 'high' position in respect of persons. The new Department was to acquire all the functions of the Treasury in relation to the universities, the research councils, the national museums and the Arts Council, and was to absorb the functions of the Office of the Minister for Science, which included several things Robbins had not mentioned, such as the Atomic Energy Authority and licensing exploitation of gravel pits. It would also take in the entire charge of the existing Ministry of Education, which was, of course, confined to England and Wales, whereas the new responsibilities conferred on it were nationwide. The University Grants Committee was to continue in relation to the new Department, but for universities alone: the overarching Higher Education Commission proposed by Robbins was lost in the mist.

Looking back, I think a great mistake was made in not considering this proposal more closely, and an opportunity of avoiding much future trouble may have been lost. If all higher education had been brought within the scope of such a commission modelled on the traditions of the UGC, it would have mattered very little that it should be linked to the state through a Department of Education and Science, since that Department would have had no 'sector' of higher education of its own to consider and develop. At that particular time, when all was in the melting pot, such a solution might just have been practicable. True, it would have meant major surgery on the Ministry of Education and surrender by the existing clients of the UGC of their particular window: but both these propositions had the authority of Robbins. Unfortunately the Robbins Report and the subsequent discussion put too much emphasis on the ministerial and departmental arrangements, and especially on the creation of a ministry which would have no real responsibilities except to receive and satisfy the proposals of advisory bodies, and as such could have no real friend in Whitehall. Indeed, even if the Robbins solution had been adopted (and it would not have lasted long if it had been, for ministries have no guarantee of survival) it would have left the real problem of two separately administered 'sectors' unsolved. The idea of a separate ministry was shadow, the idea of an overarching Higher Education Commission on the model developed by the UGC was substance, and the attractions of being able to resolve the problems of coordination within such a commission were, and are, very great.

The result was that the UGC and its flock became a specific group within the educational system. A collection of institutions which had little in common except the channel through which they received state support acquired a new formal coherence. Considered in detail the Grant List of 1965,[4] which has not changed since, has some analogies in its variety with the states composing the Holy Roman Empire, for Oxford was no more like Bradford than Bavaria was like Hesse-Darmstadt. Several were not strictly speaking universities at all, such as the two business schools and the University of Manchester Institute, or the components of the University of Wales. Little Lampeter was on the list, but components of the University of London many times its size received their grant through the university. Nor did the list correspond with the list of institutions whose heads had seats on the Committee of Vice-Chancellors and Principals, which included the Open University: but the Open University, was developed outside the UGC system. All this needs to be remembered as a warning against easy generalisations about 'the university sector'.[5]

There was at this time a nasty scuffle about the museums, galleries and Arts Council, which the Treasury showed some inclination to retain. 'Come, come,' said Sir Maurice Dean, 'you swear you won't keep the UGC as a mistress any more, and you're going to be as pure

---

[4] That year saw the addition of nine out of the ten former CATs (the tenth became a college of London University), Heriot Watt, Strathclyde, Stirling and the two business schools, bringing the number to 52. The other 39 were: Oxford and Cambridge; London; Manchester, UMIST, Leeds, Liverpool, Durham, Sheffield, Hull, Nottingham, Birmingham, Bristol, Reading, Southampton, Exeter, Newcastle, Leicester and Keele; the six university colleges of the University of Wales, plus the central body of the university itself; the 'new universities' of Sussex, Kent, York, Lancaster, Warwick, East Anglia and Essex; and the Scottish universities of St Andrews, Glasgow, Aberdeen, Edinburgh and Dundee.
[5] The difficulty of saying exactly what a university was is shown by a small incident in 1962 when international games for universities were held and the UGC was asked to advise what institutions could be regarded as providing teams or players from British universities. The only answer that could be thought of was that they would have to be from institutions on the UGC grant list. This (at that time) excluded the colleges of advanced technology, including Loughborough, which had a course in physical education and perhaps the best sporting facilities of any higher education institution in the country.

as driven snow, but you won't be happy if you can't have one or two little milliners round the corner. It won't wash, Otto, it won't wash.'

The 'high' concession was that the new Department should have two coequal Permanent Secretaries, each of whom would be an Accounting Officer,[6] one for the existing Ministry of Education functions and the other for those which were to be added. Sir Maurice Dean,[7] whose shortlived influence was exerted at these decisive moments, was assigned to the second of these posts. He was posted to the Treasury as a supernumerary Second Secretary within a fortnight of the appearance of the Robbins Report and I was immediately made responsible to him for the universities. Simultaneously he became responsible, under Lord Hailsham, for the Office of the Minister for Science.

Dean's style had been formed in the Service Departments and there was nothing of the educationalist about him. He gave a general impression of brisk, tough pinkness. He was short and broad, crisply and smartly dressed, with a dazzling white shirt and bright red braces, which he was fond of displaying by removing his jacket whenever possible.

He was a man of great courage and acuteness, and possessed unusual address and presence of mind. He throve on crises, large and small, and had the gift of timing. He could bring a patient argument to ruins by waiting till the others round the table had begun to get bored with it. 'But, Otto,' I heard him say at one such decisive moment, when a long disquisition was just ending, 'it's all done by mirrors.' I have no doubt that in that particular argument Otto was intellectually right; but the decision went against him, and politically he was in the wrong.

Dean was no idealist in business, and he was suspicious of those who seemed to him too earnest and committed. He found several in the old Ministry of Education, and they reminded him, he once said,

---

[6] The Accounting Officer is the senior permanent official of a department, and as such is personally responsible to Parliament (through the Public Accounts Committee) for his department's expenditure. This uncomfortable position provides Permanent Secretaries with considerable strength in relation to their Ministers since they can, in extremity, record dissent in writing from a ministerial direction if they consider it to be outside parliamentary authority. It also gives them grounds for insisting on scrutiny of any expenditure for which their departments are directly responsible. The Robbins Committee had shown great interest in the question, in view of its anxiety to preserve the position by which the universities were insulated from parliamentary accountability. The Helsby solution did this.

[7] 1906–78. A Wrangler at Cambridge. Entered Air Ministry 1929; Deputy Secretary of the Control Office, Germany 1943–8; Deputy Secretary Ministry of Defence 1948–52; Second Secretary Board of Trade 1952–5; Permanent Secretary Air Ministry 1955–63; Treasury (Shadow DES) 1963–4 and Joint Permanent Secretary DES April to October 1964; Permanent Secretary Ministry of Technology 1964–6.

of the Roundheads in the picture 'When Did You Last See Your Father?'

It would be equally true to say he was unimpressed by the mystique of the universities, yet I would classify him (in spite of his Salvationist connexion) as tending to the high church in the controversies that followed his appointment. Certainly no one could have fought more manfully for the universities in the crucial year following Robbins. The quinquennial settlement for 1962–7 which had been so recently and painfully negotiated was reopened for the increased numbers; a huge capital programme covering eighteen months from April 1964 was pushed through against passionate Treasury resistance; and the staff and status of the UGC was considerably strengthened, notably by negotiating a higher rank in Whitehall for its Chairman, who was now Sir John Wolfenden, Murray having declined a third term.[8]

Although Dean and I remained technically on the staff of the Treasury for a month or two after Robbins reported, a curtain between us and the main body of the Treasury was immediately lowered. I ceased to be a professional critic of expansion, and became its advocate, though even so it was necessary to moderate the passion of the innumerable clients. The cry on every side was for more universities. Some forty towns up and down the country – Scarborough, I seem to remember, was among them, and Perth, and Inverness – had launched university promotion committees. Country houses with ample parks were everywhere on offer. It was one of my earliest functions to settle with the Secretary of the UGC (by then Copleston) that all except the Scots should receive a letter saying that no new designations were intended in the immediate future.

The Universities Branch of which I was now head in the DES was in the process of formation, the first arrival being Charles Freedman, who arrived on promotion to Assistant Secretary from the Customs and Excise, to which he ultimately returned and rose to be a Commissioner. He had read physics. He was soon followed by Geoffrey Caston, originally a member of the Colonial Office but by that time working for its successor, the Department of Technical Cooperation.[9] The

[8] Till then the Chairman and Secretary of the UGC had both been (in Treasury terminology) Third Secretaries, thus balancing the inward and outward facing sides of the office. The Chairman still ranks as a Second Secretary, but the Secretaryship has recently been regraded a rank lower than formerly, at Undersecretary.

[9] Later Secretary of the Schools Council, Registrar of Oxford University, Secretary General of the Committee of Vice-Chancellors and Principals, and (now) Vice-Chancellor of the University of the South Pacific.

Branch, which stayed unchanged for some time, was an interesting one because its senior members were comparatively young and brought fresh minds to their work from Departments which were not imbued by the educational world. The third, and last, Assistant Secretary to join it was a non-graduate from the Treasury, David Skidmore, who was to retire early from the service to become a Congregationalist minister. When things settled down Charles Freedman did Student Support, David Skidmore did Finance, and Geoffrey Caston all the other things.

We were not allowed to stay in Great George Street for long, and before Christmas 1963 we removed to the ruinous grandeur of Richmond Terrace just across the road, which already housed the Office of the Minister for Science. Dean bounded round with officials from the Ministry of Works demanding renovations, and actually got some; but they were sketchy, since it was then the unspoken policy of the Ministry of Works to demolish the crumbling structure altogether and use the site for something else. Somewhat against the Treasury's grain we insisted before we left on copying all the Treasury files about universities for the past ten years. The demand was unanswerable.

Buildings can be very important. Richmond Terrace might be shabby but it was in the heart of Whitehall and was neither the Treasury nor the Ministry of Education, located as it then was in Curzon Street, Mayfair. For some time we remained far closer to those of our colleagues who were concerned with scientific research than with the educationalists: and much was happening in the organisation of research.

The old Department of Scientific and Industrial Research was in process of being superseded under the scheme which was put into effect by the Science and Technology Act 1965. This formalised something of great importance to the universities, namely 'the dual support system'.

The Robbins Report does not directly refer to these major changes then being planned for the research council structure. Nevertheless it describes the main features of what has since taken shape in the dual support doctrine, whose essence is that while universities, using the block grant provided by the UGC, provide the general facilities needed for research, particular grants are available from the separately financed research councils to provide the specialised services and equipment needed for projects judged to be of 'timeliness and promise'. The UGC thus deals with universities and universities alone: the research councils with university departments and individual researchers. The system thus brought two different approaches, as well as two different sources of public funds, into the financing of universities. One was based on the general health of the university and its ability to provide library facilities, laboratories and above all a measure of staff time for a research base. The other depended on a judgment of which plants growing from that soil deserved particular encouragement.

The Science and Technology Act established four research councils – for science, for medicine, for agriculture and for the natural environment – together with an overarching Council for Scientific Policy which distributed a science budget between them. Very soon a fifth was added: the Social Science Research Council. A committee under Lord Heyworth, the Chairman of Unilever, had been appointed to consider such a development during the latter part of the time the Robbins Committee was in session. The climate was favourable, and so was the Heyworth Report. There were some sceptical reactions within Whitehall, mainly on the ground that such research was better commissioned *ad hoc* in relation to particular social problems, rather than left solely to academic choice; but these doubts made little impression after the general election of 1964. The new body was rapidly constituted on the same model as its scientific sisters, and since social science needed, in comparison with them, quite modest expenditure on capital or equipment, the effect of this new source of funds on the number of projects and researchers in social science was spectacular.[10]

The significance of the dual support system for the universities was (and is) heightened by the doctrine that since students reading for higher degrees make important contributions to research and provide the workforce for many research projects, their funding should be the responsibility of the research councils in their respective fields. The approved system for doing this in the natural sciences is to allocate quotas of studentships to particular university departments, which the departments then fill for themselves. This system, after much debate, was extended to the Social Science Research Council, but not, of course, to the humanities, because there was no research council to handle

---

[10] Lord Robbins himself was deeply interested in this development and made the suggestion that the British Academy (of which he was then President) should undertake the task, rather than a research council. I doubt if that would have been practicable, at any rate at that time. The Academy has, however, since expanded to provide research support from Government funds to the only large area not covered by the research councils – namely the humanities.

it. In that area a national competition for postgraduate awards was held annually under the aegis of the Education Departments.[11]

The dual support system was and is a very effective way of reconciling the autonomy implied in the block grant with the need for some guidance over the direction of nationally funded research; but it is not without its problems and strains. Research grants are for a time only, and when they come to an end the activity they supported must either lapse or be absorbed into the general financing of the university as a claim on its block grant. It is indeed the logic of the system that the resources of the research councils should constantly move on to fresh projects, and that those which have run their course – whether to success or failure – should be wound up. But in human terms this is far from easy to arrange. From being protected by separate funding, successive groups of specialised staff find themselves faced at best with competition and at worst with redundancy; for even if general university funding is sufficient to rescue them in their hour of need, it can hardly be expected to provide it for every activity launched on a temporary basis. If UGC grant for any reason – say a levelling off of student numbers – ceases to expand, worse difficulties will occur, especially if spending by the research councils (which is always attractive to Governments because it is 'mission-oriented') has been high. Matters become still more serious if the 'base' provided by the UGC in the shape of laboratories, libraries and equipment becomes eroded or obsolete, since this makes it difficult for the outside agencies to launch new projects.

But much in the centre of 'implementing Robbins' was still wreathed in uncertainty and passion. The Report had recommended the founding of six more universities (one of which was to be in Scotland); five prestigious and amply financed technological institutions; two new business schools; and the elevation of the ten colleges of advanced technology to university status. This programme would have added twenty-one institutions to an existing UGC grant list of about thirty. Moreover it seemed as if the grant list might be perpetually kept open

---

[11] There are arguments for the quota system, but it is also open to objection. It tends over a period to get set in rigid patterns and so not to leave room for new developments. It places much power in the hands of the departments with the largest quotas, and may tend to favour applicants who will provide a useful pair of hands in an existing team, rather than originality. For these reasons I had serious doubts about applying it to the Social Science Research Council, particularly because of the doctrinal basis of many social science projects and their consequent attraction for the like-minded. I had anxious discussions with the first Chairman of the SSRC (Michael Young) on the subject. The quota system for social science has now been partially abandoned.

to promotion (but not relegation). Huge sums of money were at stake, and the control of public expenditure was flapping in the wind.

Into all this came the political convulsion following Mr Macmillan's illness and resignation. Lord Hailsham, who had become responsible for carrying out the Government's commitments on the Robbins Report, was one of the principal contenders for the succession. Nothing could have shown (except what was going to happen next) more clearly the political position higher education had come, for a moment, to occupy. Lord Hailsham led a debate on the Robbins Report in the House of Lords which is one of the most impressive deliberations I have ever listened to.

When the Department of Education and Science came officially into existence in April 1964, Sir Quintin Hogg (as he had by then become) was appointed its founding Secretary of State. Sir Edward Boyle, who till then had been Minister of Education and, as such, a member of the Cabinet, gallantly accepted the second place in the new organisation. It was a further bow in the direction of 'two-Minister' solution advocated in the Robbins Report.

The higher education side of the new Department immediately took over responsibility for the colleges of advanced technology, then still on direct grant through annual line-by-line budgeting in direct negotiation with departmental officials. All of them had massive building programmes, and several were planning to move to new sites, thus presenting almost the same problems as completely new universities.[12]

Only one completely new university was eventually designated. This was Stirling, the new university which had been promised to Scotland.[13] The reasons were political, not academic, for the expansion recommended in Scotland could easily have been accomplished by the existing universities together with the Glasgow College of Technology and the Heriot Watt College, both of which were already accorded university status; and the independent Dundee, already planned.

Even at that time, and certainly with hindsight, 'green fields' appeared as a slow and expensive form of provision, and it was hardly

[12] Bristol was to move to Bath; Brunel to Uxbridge; Battersea to Guildford; Aston was to be redeveloped elsewhere in Birmingham, and Bradford proposed a new site which was troubled by the possibility of subsidence attributable to the existence of unrecorded mining works. The plans for Salford involved a most successful restructuring of the centre of the town and the conversion of the polluted river Irwell into an agreeable stretch of water flowing through a pleasant park, in which the hideous Victorian technical college building from which the institution had sprung was carefully preserved.
[13] Immense interest was mounted for a major technological institution on Teesside. The plans were too ambitious, yet I saw them fail with some regret.

the right response to what had been claimed as an emergency. It spread resources – ample though they were – much too thin. Central buildings, especially libraries, had to be provided at more places than was necessary, and in many cases the lack of hinterland whence students could work from home or in which they could find adequate lodgings, called for a great deal of purpose-built student residence. Above all, it preempted resources for many years ahead in order to bring the new institutions to a practical and economic size. Extra students who could have been accommodated at modest cost in the larger and stronger institutions had to be diverted, if possible, to new, smaller ones at higher cost, even when resources began to shrink.

Excellent academic results have been achieved at the 'Universities of Noddyland' (an unkind phrase which escaped from Sir Maurice Dean during this period), but it is difficult to see any reason why they could not have been achieved elsewhere.[14] So a high price was paid for innovation in a new place, excitement and novelty of atmosphere. Really good foci usually emerge unexpectedly, and what is planned as a dramatic centrepiece can often turn out to be a cumbersome disappointment. The argument that a new site with a fresh start made it possible to escape from the rigidities of the older institutions seems to me limited. Every institution, once it has grown to an effective size, will develop its rigidities, whether it has been in existence for twenty years or two hundred: and *coelum non animum mutant qui trans mare currunt*.

Several of the colleges of advanced technology, also moving to green fields, sought green subjects to go with them. But as existing institutions they already had large staffs, many of whom had joined long before the arrival of CAT status, and all these were now on their way to being university teachers, with time built into their schedules for research. There was a sift, but not many were affected. It would have been inhuman to halt teachers in mid-career because their institution was to be designated a university and they then, after years of loyal and adequate service, did not pass an unlooked-for test. The Robbins Report provided no guidance, and the matter was solved with as little pain as possible.

But there was to be collective, if not individual pain. The former

---

[14] Instances of successful foci at new universities: marine biology at Stirling; mediaeval history at York; topology at Warwick; south–east Asian studies at Kent; comparative religion at Lancaster; development studies at Sussex.

CATs found the freedom conferred by the block grant dispensed by the UGC much more difficult to live with than the detailed but ultimately generous budgeting of the Department. With the Department one could even come back for more in the course of year if one was short; but not with the quinquennial system of the UGC, which looked so liberal to those outside it. Indeed those direct grant institutions which were not CATs and had also been assigned to the UGC by Robbins (the College of Aeronautics and the Royal College of Art) were quick to perceive this, and clung to departmental finance, while at the same time obtaining all the outward trappings of university status.

Of the other additions to the university world proposed by the Robbins Report only two were founded: the business schools of London and Manchester. There was more pressure on their behalf than for any of the other novelties, and there was a feeling, too, that here at least part of the cost would be borne by the direct beneficiaries – business itself and the individuals receiving the prestigious qualifications the schools would bestow. Nevertheless the direct subsidy was large and the initial industrial support ebbed away in the decades that followed. The teacups bounced on the table with the impact of Lord Robens of Wolsingham's fist reinforcing his requirement that the UGC capital grant should allow for a bathroom for every student of the London Business School. The UGC had thought one for every four would be generous.

All discussion was held in the pervasive atmosphere that everything was to be provided through public funds. It was contrary to the scale of things to discuss student numbers in figures of less than a thousand, or finance in sums under a million: hence, no doubt, the hesitation of Whitehall about new ventures. But along with this, in Whitehall as elsewhere, there was a determination that the system should not be devalued as a result of expansion. Robbins was not done on the cheap. Building standards were generous, staffing ratios were maintained or even allowed to improve, postgraduate support was rapidly extended, and the growth of ancillary services (health, counselling, placement, sport) was faster than the growth of student numbers.

All this was accompanied by rapid unionisation of those who provided these and other non-teaching services in universities which in the years before Robbins had been comparatively small patriarchal employers of the workforce they needed in addition to their academic staff. Suddenly, and at a time of full employment, the universities entered the market for thousands of technicians, administrators, clerical workers

63

of all sorts, library assistants, porters and storemen, cooks, waitresses, cleaners and gardeners. At first each recruit had his or her own terms, but unions were not slow to organise this new industry, and gradually the university managements created an organisation of employers. The Robbins Report had envisaged the Committee of Vice-Chancellors and Principals as developing into a kind of university parliament, but contains no hint that one of its most important functions would be as an employers' organisation for an industry whose total numbers (including academic staff) are hard to determine, but cannot today be much short of 100,000 employees. There can be no doubt that the non-academic development of university staff has cost considerably more than any figure which could have been reckoned on evidence available to the Robbins Committee, if such had been tendered. But no such calculation was made.

Immense progress was made under Sir John Wolfenden in the summer of 1964 in equipping the UGC for its new task. To relieve the Chairman of what was becoming an intolerable burden, two Deputy Chairmen were appointed.[15] The number of Undersecretaries was raised from one to two, and of Assistant Secretaries from two to four. A large group of architects and quantity surveyors was assembled to extract maximum value from the capital programme. Altogether the staff was doubled, and the office was moved from its traditional quarters in Belgrave Square to Park Crescent. Comprehensive information about the land held by universities was assembled, and this was followed in due course by a survey of all their buildings. The most important move of all, however, was on the academic side.

Almost since its foundation the UGC had had a Medical Sub-Committee which, though not all-powerful (its proposals sometimes encountered choppy water when they came to the main Committee), was in many respects the UGC so far as the medical schools were concerned. Wolfenden's reform was to extend the sub-committee system to all university subjects to provide, as he put it, 'eyes and ears'. There were thirteen eyes and ears altogether, each presided over by a member of the Committee, and, like the Committee itself, peripatetic. But whereas until then the Committee could at best spend a day or two at each

---

[15] An experiment that was soon abandoned. It was difficult to find a satisfying role for the Deputy Chairman since the Chairman, great as is the burden of his office, cannot delegate his personal position as the mediator of the university world. In the end *ad hoc* delegation to the longer-serving members of the Committee proved a more effective way of helping the Chairman; and from 1973 onwards an annual Vice-Chairman was informally designated, largely to provide for occasions when the Chairman was temporarily unable to act.

university every five years, the visitations of thirteen sub-committees, which included membership from outside the main Committee, ensured that one side or another of each university came under much more frequent and well-informed scrutiny.

These changes were backed up by a steadily improved plan of statistical information, removing for ever the reproach that the UGC was a remote, amateurish body which relied on obsolete and imperfect data. Here the Robbins Report had set a standard to be maintained and improved. From the 'high church' point of view the data base may have become almost too good, but it certainly became one of the best in Whitehall.

When, in October 1964, Mr Wilson gained power with the slenderest of majorities, he had already given much thought to higher education, which, along with the connected subject of science and technology, figured prominently in the Labour manifesto. He had also contributed personally the idea of the Open University (originally christened by him the University of the Air), though it did not emerge in quite the shape he had originally proposed.[16] More broadly he saw higher education as needing to be more closely integrated with economic and industrial affairs, with the various ministries concerned (Education and Science, Economic Affairs, and Technology) as needing to act in concert and in the national interest. The attitude of the new regime was, in fact, 'low' rather than 'high', and much time was consumed at meetings in which officers of the Department of Education and Science such as myself pointed out how Government policy imposed limitations on the intervention in the educational system proposed by officials committed to the cause of organising technology.

The most extreme kind of intervention took the form of 'manpower planning', either for particular groups (more town planners, more statisticians) or generally. There is now, I think, fairly widespread agreement that the central control of the numbers in which particular kinds of academic performance are produced by the educational system is impracticable, and perhaps conceptually unsound. Any such plan must depend on a forecast of numbers needed several years hence, when facilities will have been provided and the education given to the

[16] The original prescription was based on television, and its then novel powers and there was a strong implication that as compared with a traditional residential university greater cost-effectiveness would be achieved. The development was, of course, over and above the growth in higher education proposed by the Robbins Committee. Television is now an important prop, but from the beginning it was clear that the strength of the venture lay in correspondence courses and local tutorial groups on a national scale.

students, so mismatching is all but inevitable if the exercise is attempted in any but the most general way.[17]

More fundamentally, however, the notion depends upon prior agreement about the scale on which each service is to be both provided and staffed over a long future period. These are questions that go far beyond educational planning.

Michael Stewart was the first Labour Secretary of State, but passed rapidly from Curzon Street to replace the discomfited Patrick Gordon Walker at the Foreign Office. He was succeeded by Anthony Crosland, who was perhaps better fitted for the post than any of his successors, and was well suited for the times through which it was passing. He was adventurous, enthusiastic and confident like a man who feels a strong horse between his knees. His abilities were very great, and he was the heir, the triumphant product, of the Oxford School of PPE in the 1930s. He was a democrat and a pluralist.

As his deputy for higher education he had Lord Bowden, advanced to the peerage and given leave of absence from his post as Principal of the University of Manchester Institute of Technology. He came to office with fixed, yet disparate ideas, which were strongly imprinted on his mind but did not make up (so far as I could see) a coherent whole, though each of them had some appeal. On being appointed, his first visit was to the Chairman of the UGC, Sir John Wolfenden, to whom he imparted his views and said that he proposed from time to time to take the chair of the University Grants Committee. Sir John demurred, and suggested that before proceeding further the new Minister should make the acquaintance of the Permanent Secretary. This Lord Bowden promptly did, presenting himself to the porter at Richmond Terrace and inquiring for Sir Maurice Dean – but not before Sir John had spoken to Sir Maurice, who was at that moment presiding over a meeting of officials on computer policy. On the entry of Lord Bowden Dean rose with a sweeping bow and invited him to take the chair he himself had just been occupying.

Lord Bowden never understood the concept of being advised. Advice may be accepted or refused or not invited at all: but an honest adviser cannot be expected to modify his advice to suit the preconceptions

[17] A relevant example was quoted to me at an international conference on the subject by a distinguished Polish economist. In order to man a large programme to restore and conserve historic buildings a five-year course for art historians was established. It took about seven years for the first graduate to emerge (allowing for time taken to recruit staff and plan the course). By that time budgetary considerations had caused the programme of restoration to be heavily cut, and most of the art historians had to find jobs elsewhere.

of the person advised. Lord Bowden did not see the civil service as a system of advice: he saw it as a machine for giving effect to his existing views, as holding keys and controlling levers which were inaccessible to him personally, but which should be exerted in response to his opinions.

In the autumn of 1964, after nine crowded months and observing that it was a bit hard at his time of life to have to start yet another thing off with an up-turned barrel, Sir Maurice Dean departed to become Permanent Secretary of the Ministry of Technology under Frank Cousins. He was succeeded by Sir Bruce Fraser,[18] who left the permanent secretaryship of the Ministry of Health with understandable reluctance.

The juggernaut on Robbins principles rattled along, but one great question was still to be resolved. The ragged edge of university status or, to change the metaphor, the ladder from the technical college to paradise which Robbins had left leaning against the wall, still disturbed the educational world. That problem was not to be solved at Richmond Terrace but at Curzon Street.

---

[18] Born 1910. Double First at Cambridge in classics and English. Entered civil service in the Scottish Office 1933; Treasury 1936–60 (Third Secretary 1956–60); Deputy Secretary Ministry of Aviation 1960; Permanent Secretary Ministry of Health 1960–4; Joint Permanent Secretary DES 1964–5; Permanent Secretary Ministry of Land and Natural Resources 1965–6; Comptroller and Auditor General 1966–71. Revised Sir Ernest Gower's *Plain Words* 1973.

VI

The Rift in the Lute

Sir Bruce Fraser, before becoming Permanent Secretary of the Ministry of Health, had been Otto's predecessor in charge of the part of the Treasury which was concerned with universities. He shared Sir Edward Bridges' 'high-church' attitude to that aspect of the Treasury's responsibilities, thoroughly understood the traditions of the University Grants Committee, and had played a considerable and sympathetic part in the plans for expanding the universities that had preceded the appointment of the Robbins Committee. Nevertheless, after controlling a complete department with conspicuous success, the move to control half a department neither stretched nor satisfied him. Indeed the 'Robbins' half of the Department of Education and Science was by this time even less viable than it had been at the outset, for a good deal of the science-aligned work had departed with Sir Maurice Dean to the new Ministry of Technology.

The atmosphere at DES during those early months of the Wilson Government was feverish and Sir Bruce Fraser's highly intellectual and sensitive character was not adapted to it. Three ministries – two of them newly created – shared responsibility for the policy of applying science and technology to the service of the community. Men who had held positions in the university world – such as Lords Bowden, Snow, Blackett and Balogh – were now stationed in or close to educational policy, and their instinctive wish was at last to use Government authority to impel education in directions they had always advocated. The job of protecting the independence of the institutions (which everyone accepted in principle) bore heavily on the UGC and the Education Departments, who consequently incurred accusations of unresponsiveness. In addition to this, and to the administration of the massive programme of expansion already under way, was the Open University, which was at first assigned to the higher-education side of the bi-focal DES – I think I wrote the first minute on the subject. But it was soon moved to the other half of the Department, where Jennie Lee was located as the Junior Minister with special responsibility for the project and direct access to the Prime Minister; and throughout its

68

planning stages it was developed quite separately from all the rest of higher and further education.

The other half of the bi-focal Department was now headed by Sir Herbert Andrew, who had recently arrived from the Board of Trade.[1] He shared Sir Maurice Dean's quality of coolness in a crisis, but not his cheerful rather cynical aggressiveness. Dean belonged by training and instinct to the world of direct administration, and was by temperament an interventionist. Sir Herbert's natural tendency accorded with the traditions of the Department in which he had till then spent his career, which were to intervene as little as possible and stand in readiness to manage crises. The failure of the first negotiations for Britain to enter the Common Market, in which he had been much concerned, had come as a deep disappointment to him, whereas Dean, in similar circumstances, would simply have turned a shade pinker and gone on to something else. Andrew is the wisest and kindest of the Permanent Secretaries in this story: but also, under his grey and modest manner, very cool and firm.

Sir Herbert's inclination not to interfere too much suited the non-interventionist traditions of Curzon Street which I have described in Chapter II, but not the mounting external pressure for 'purposiveness' and 'planning'. There were, however, certain parts of the Curzon Street machine where such pressures had already found a friendlier reception. The creation of the directly administered colleges of advanced technology and the 'master-minding' of the Council for National Academic Awards[2] were striking instances of Curzon Street initiative. Two zones of the Department were especially active in this forward policy. The Inspectors concerned with further education had for some time formed a distinct corps within the Inspectorate as a whole, and the developments in technical education just mentioned had been very much of their making: and they exercised a very detailed control over the approval of courses and the distribution of scientific equipment. Secondly,

[1] Sir Herbert Andrew, born 1910. After reading science at Oxford, entered the Patent Office as an Assistant Examiner in 1931; Board of Trade 1936–63 (Second Secretary 1955–63); UK delegation to the Common Market Conference 1961–3; Permanent Secretary Ministry of Education and Joint (later sole) Permanent Under Secretary DES 1963–70.

Since 1944 only one Permanent Secretary of the Ministry of Education and its successor the DES (Sir William Pile) has been a career officer of that Department. This does not indicate lack of talent among those who have served there, since more than one has risen to be a Permanent Secretary elsewhere; it indicates the constant itch to make the education system more 'responsive'.

[2] The credit for this, the indispensable underpinning of the non-university part of the 'binary system' which was now just round the corner, largely belongs to the gentle and serious J. A. R. Pimlott, then an Undersecretary.

the Architects and Buildings Branch, under a succession of outstanding professional and administrative chiefs, had obtained a considerable grip not only over the distribution of the capital programme but over the technical means of achieving it through new building methods. The chief representative of the positive line of development in higher education was T.R. (now Sir Toby) Weaver, the Deputy Secretary at Curzon Street since 1962.

Sir Toby Weaver's opinions and character are probably better known than those of any other senior official concerned with higher education during those years, so it is unnecessary for me to pay my tribute to them here, especially as I was his close colleague over a long period. Of his achievements, however, it is necessary to say something.

The problem faced by Weaver and those responsible for higher education outside the universities was the impossible situation in which the Robbins Report and subsequent decisions left that subject by seeking to brigade the teacher colleges with the universities and treating the technical colleges as a kind of sump from which any elements of distinction would (by methods not explained) be advanced to university status. It is perfectly true that many of the existing universities had originated at humbler levels; but their advance had been achieved over a long period of laissez-faire. In the aftermath of the Robbins Report the expectation was for a system, and therefore a system for institutional promotion. The Department was besieged with applicants from the more prominent technical colleges for advancement into the autonomous world.

This prospect of continued turbulence among the technical colleges was complicated by two other factors. What would happen to the work which those promoted would shed on their departure into autonomy? Their part-time and evening courses, their teaching of those not aspiring to degrees, their character as local institutions? All this would have to survive in new or truncated colleges if the old ones became universities. Secondly, even if a world of laissez-faire could accommodate an indefinitely increasing number of autonomous institutions of higher education, was this practicable where the autonomous institutions themselves were conceived as a national system financed by the national exchequer and enjoying, supposedly, parity of esteem?

The larger trees in this jungle had been felled by decisions announced in December 1964 and February 1965. The first of these rejected the proposal of the Robbins Report that all the teacher-training colleges should be absorbed into the universities: a foregone conclusion, already

70

reached by the out-going Government. The second announcement swept away the recommendation for six more new universities and three specially enriched institutions of science and technology – those for which their begetter, Sir Patrick Linstead, had coined the ingenious acronym SISTERS.[3]

What, then, was to happen in the world of further education, to which the Robbins Committee had allotted only a comparatively small part of the expansion it proposed? It was a question that had to be settled in a way that did not destroy the further education system or subject it to endless ambition and frustration over advancement to university status on a selective basis.

It must be remembered that the one great interest which had not received the Robbins Report with unreserved rapture was that of the local education authorities. They had already seen the colleges of advanced technology – originally colleges of their own – taken into direct grant and then turned into universities. They had earlier seen the redbrick universities, of which some of them had been so proud, become part of the national system. The system of mandatory student support had put local revenues at the service of that national system which was now to be enormously expanded. Such control as they had ever had over the students they paid to send to the university had been taken away – a subject on which Sir William Alexander[4] often waxed eloquent. They were not going to see more ground given up without a struggle. The general financial support the universities had once had from neighbouring authorities (it had been 10 per cent of total university income before the War) had accordingly shrunk to a trickle.[5]

[3] Special Institutions of Scientific and Technological Education and Research. There were to have been five, two of which already existed in Imperial College and the University of Manchester Institute of Science and Technology, while a third was to be developed in Glasgow and has become the University of Strathclyde. One of the remaining two was to be completely new, and the other produced out of 'a selected College of Advanced Technology.' All, the Robbins Report urged, should have 'financial support similar to that given to the Imperial College during the past decade' and have 'good staffing ratios, a liberal proportion of senior to junior posts, and adequate provision of equipment and technical assistance'. Here the Committee took leave of its insistence on parity of treatment and its strictures on Oxford and Cambridge for their unduly attractive qualities.

[4] The creator, and for many years the Secretary, of the Association of Education Committees. With his death it melted away.

[5] The anxieties of the local education authorities were shared, and indeed given a shape, by the Association of Teachers in Technical Institutions in their policy statement 'The Future of Technical Education Within the Higher Education System,' which appeared about the same time as the Woolwich speech. This speaks of 'the tradition of following knowledge wherever it beckons, the emphasis upon institutional independence and the unwillingness to allow outside interests to influence the curriculum' as being characteristic

One solution to the problem would have been to emphasise the vital importance of the work done by the colleges outside the range of Robbins's preoccupation with full-time students working for degrees; and to group the degree-level work of the colleges academically round the local university, while leaving the management of the colleges firmly – nay irrevocably – in the hands of the local education authorities. Such a solution would have been gritty and unspectacular, with built-in tensions. It would not have been impracticable.

In Whitehall the answer had to be found by those responsible for further education, not those responsible for universities, and the text of the speech delivered by Anthony Crosland at Woolwich on 27 April 1965 was not, so far as I know, communicated to the UGC beforehand, or made the subject of their advice. It would not have been regarded as their business. I can remember being in Crosland's room that evening, on some other business, and seeing the dinner-jacketed party on the point of departure. There was a sense of occasion about them and, I thought, a sense of anxiety.

The key passage in the speech needs to be quoted:

On the one hand we have what has come to be called the autonomous sector,[6] represented by the universities, in whose ranks, of course, I now include the colleges of advanced technology. On the other hand, we have the public sector, represented by the leading technical colleges and the colleges of education. The Government accepts this dual system as being fundamentally the right one, with each sector making its own distinctive contribution to the whole. . . . We prefer the dual system for four basic reasons.

First, there is an ever increasing need and demand for vocational, professional, and industrially based courses in higher education. . . . This demand cannot be fully met by the universities . . . it therefore requires a separate sector with a separate tradition and outlook. . . . Secondly . . . if the universities have a 'class' monopoly as degree-giving bodies and if every college which achieves high standards moves automatically into the University Club, then the residual public sector becomes a permanent poor relation. . . . This must be bad for morale, bad for standards, and productive only of an unhealthy rat-race mentality. Thirdly, it is desirable in itself that a substantial part of the higher education system should be under social control, directly responsible to social needs. . . . Fourthly . . . why should we not aim at . . . a vocationally oriented non-university sector which is degree-giving and with an appropriate amount of postgraduate work and opportunities for learning comparable with those of the universities, and giving a first-class

of universities, and 'not easily reconciled with professional oriented courses in which theory and practice are closely interlocked'. This looks impressive until one considers that medicine is a university subject, and that 'outside intervention in the curriculum' is traditionally resented as much in other parts of education as in the universities.
[6] The word 'sector' originates (in this case) in the Robbins Report itself: see the heading to Table 44 (p. 160), 'Places Needed in Full-time Higher Education: by Sectors'.

professional training? Between [these sectors] we want ... mutual understanding and healthy rivalry where their work overlaps.

This certainly built an effective barrier against technical college aspirations in the direction of autonomy. It said what is undoubtedly true – namely that it is perfectly possible to carry on higher education without the privileges of autonomy and freedom from public audit to which Robbins attached such high importance. But it did a great deal more than this, by fortifying and adorning the barrier with institutional doctrines which constituted a kind of Robbins in reverse. A 'low' rhetoric now confronted the 'high' rhetoric of the Robbins Report, and the Government adopted both.

It is odd to reflect that those who had argued most passionately in favour of the 'seamless robe' at the time of that controversy, maintaining, in the words of Mr Shearman, that 'education is one and indivisible', now inserted a seam of their own. Shearman's own words – and his note of reservation is in my view among the wisest documents penned on the subject – suggested that the consequence of an administrative separation in education would be 'that each will be fighting for his own hand and both may suffer'. He was speaking of the proposal for two Ministers, but the words are equally applicable in this case:

With this thought of the unity of education uppermost, I should wish to see the universities take up a position of leadership and inspiration which would promote the health of all, by identifying themselves with the whole, while maintaining as they must, the values for which they stand, and which they could do much to foster elsewhere.[7]

It is a far cry from this to binarism.

In its stated form the binary doctrine included not only the higher work of the technical colleges but the much larger area of teacher education outside the universities, for which the existing status had been preserved before the Woolwich speech was delivered. The point matters because their inclusion made the area designated as 'the public sector' seem larger than in fact it was.

The total number of places in full-time higher education proposed by the Robbins Committee and accepted as a commitment by the Conservative and Labour Governments in succession was 328,000 by 1967, and 392,000 by 1973. In this latter year the universities were to contribute 219,000 places and the colleges of education 122,000: the further education colleges in England and Wales (the problem was separately

---

[7] Robbins Report, p. 294.

dealt with in Scotland) were to contribute only 45,000, some 12½ per cent of the entire number. The growth rate assigned to them was certainly large (they mustered only 28,000 degree-level students in 1963) but it was considerably less than either of the other 'sectors' for whose expansion major capital programmes had already been agreed.

It was from these modest numbers that the 'public sector' in its generally understood sense was brigaded into polytechnics and sent over the top, rather like a last line of reserves, towards the terrain into which the colleges of advanced technology had marched, and disappeared into the mist.

But this time there was a very great difference – indeed there were many great differences. The new 'sector' now appeared to have been given a new trust and a special purpose, and if it was not to betray them it should retain the lower-level and part-time students that made up its majority. Nobody denied their importance, socially and economically. Unfortunately they had not received the attention of a major report. Whatever the doctrine, there was still a danger that in taking up the challenge of more full-time degree students the colleges designated to form the new tier would divert resources to them from their existing effort.

Secondly, bearing in mind the ample provision already being made for science and technology in the university programme, there was a serious prospect that the further education colleges would not be very effective competitors for full-time students in those subjects, but would find themselves responding instead to the surplus of applicants in social science and arts that could not find university places; and to the demand from overseas.

The third difference concerned finance. The colleges of advanced technology had received their support from the ministry, and this should in theory have given the ministry direct control over what went on in them. In practice it did not. They had their own management structure, made their own appointments, and under the friendly guidance of the Further Education Inspectorate designed their own courses. The traditional unwillingness of the Department to become involved in directly educational matters made the CAT Directors, who were subject to far less internal restraint by way of councils and senates, more powerful in their own institutions than Vice-Chancellors in universities. Just the same the total recurrent income available to each of them from year to year was under the ministry's control. This was not going to be the case with the new wave of institutions, which

74

were to form part of the local authority education budget and attracted central funds only in proportion to what the local authorities provided. That provision, admittedly, was not made for each polytechnic by the local authority in whose area it happened to be. It was pooled, on the argument that the polytechnics – like the universities – formed a national system to which each education authority should accordingly contribute its quota: but the size of the pool was defined by the demands made on it, and was therefore not under anyone's control. There was still a great deal of detailed intervention by individual authorities over the internal affairs of 'their' individual polytechnics, but no limit to the total cost of the system. It was thus the exact converse of the system operated by the University Grants Committee.

It is surprising that the Treasury did not notice this at the time – though it was later to do so. I can only guess that Great George Street, having shed its special and rather strange responsibility for the universities, responded to a natural sympathy for studies claiming direct economic value. So the Woolwich speech constituted a bid which was all the more ingenious for being unquantified. As Sir Edward Boyle observed, the Robbins quota of some 50,000 higher education places in the technical colleges was absurdly low.[8] It followed that the new doctrine meant either an increase in the total numbers accepted on the recommendation of the Robbins Committee, or the transfer of some of those it had assigned to the 'autonomous sector' to the newly evoked 'public sector'.

The style of the Woolwich speech – which owed much to Mr Crosland himself – was designed to point the sharpest possible outline of the virtues claimed for the new tier of institutions, and I am sure that in the writing of it there was no intention of casting a shadow on the universities. Nevertheless this was inevitably what it did, even when it recited their glories and truth-seeking ideals. The emphasis on the words 'responsive', 'relevant' and 'socially controlled' as the characteristics of the new institutions denoted as the 'public sector' was bound to carry the implication that the 'autonomous sector' did not possess them in the same degree, and even, perhaps, that its 'autonomy' had something self-regarding about it. It was only too easy for a hearer of the Woolwich speech to see the universities as somehow

---

[8] 'On the Committee's estimate of 50,000 [degree-level] places by 1973 for the regional and area colleges Boyle said, quoting Dr Johnson, "Sir, do not let yourself be imposed upon by such an absurdity."' Sir Toby Weaver in *The Times Higher Educational Supplement*, 1 November 1983.

placed in isolation, seeking after truth, pursuing learning for its own sake, and getting a lot of money for it: and to recall the stereotype of Oxford and Cambridge. But such a shadow could not really reach those ancient, distinguished and highly adaptable universities. Instead it darkened the growth points of the university system. To describe Salford (then on its way to university status) or Leeds or for that matter the London School of Economics as 'ivory towers' is a misuse of language, and no phrase has done more harm.

Thus the 'binary doctrine' gave the attitudes I have described as 'high' and 'low' an institutional framework which hardened with time. It may well have stung, or helped to sting, the universities into seeking, ever more energetically, to make their offerings modern – though the competition between them hardly needed this stimulus; but it also introduced tensions and distortions which it has taken a long time to relieve and dispel. It emphasised stereotypes: on the one hand the traditional, unworldly don of conservative instincts, more interested in abstruse research than in teaching; and on the other the challenging radical polytechnic lecturer, with one foot in industry, another in the classroom and the third in social reform. Yet in fact the universities have been remarkably innovative in their teaching and the polytechnics have gradually, and deservedly, attracted their quota of research.

All in all the hard lines of 'binarism' were the counterparts of the exaggerations of the Robbins Report in the spheres of autonomy and non-accountability. Among the most important sources of the tragedy with which this book is concerned was the incompatibility of these notions with the other noble idea enunciated in the Report that the universities should constitute the national system of higher education. That vision, if it was not destroyed, was muffled and impaired by the Woolwich speech, which in a paradoxical way preserved the predominance of the old metropolitan universities long after their share of higher education had shrunk, and impeded the flowering of other university centres.

The Scottish Education Department faced the same administrative problem as was solved by 'binarism' in England and Wales, but did not follow the south into that doctrine. The Scottish Central Institutions (directly funded by Government) were strong technological colleges which could well, under the Robbins philosophy, have been candidates for university status. A firm restraining hand, innocent of any metaphysical doctrine, was laid upon them. 'Binarism', Sir Norman Graham[9]

[9] Permanent Secretary of the Scottish Education Department 1964–73.

and his successors were fond of saying, 'stops south of the Tweed.' Bridges between the Scottish universities and the Central Institutions were patiently constructed, though not without difficulty. That rock of offence to the Robbins Committee, the Universities (Scotland) Act 1889, survived quietly on the statute book and we are now within four years of celebrating its centenary.

Two sources of trouble of a far less theoretical nature than any so far mentioned were stored up by the Woolwich speech and the development of a new higher education 'sector'. One concerned information. Following the achievements of Claus Moser the UGC was already at work perfecting its data about the universities, and within a few years there was a reliable and comprehensive bank of information on the subject which provided a basis for both planning and criticism centrally and locally. The corresponding task for the far-flung 'public sector' has not, even now, been convincingly achieved and is, of course, far more difficult.

Secondly, the tenure, terms of service, salary scales and professional associations prevailing in the two sectors belonged to two different traditions and were utterly distinct. I have already touched on those of the university world: those of the polytechnics belonged to the statutory, highly formalised arrangements of Burnham and its cognate negotiating bodies which governed the pay and conditions of teachers in schools. University teachers, perhaps, would not have had it otherwise.

Thus two horses from different stables were placed in harness together, and from this point onwards any discussion of the universities has to give weight to the existence of the 'other sector' – whether that discussion is about fee structure, salaries, competition for research funds, or the distribution, variation and justification of student numbers. By 1970 the 'public sector' contained 150,000 full-time students at degree level (though only about one-third were in polytechnics). But that was not the point. Counting the whole of the 'public sector', including the part-time and evening work followed by millions of students, there were by 1970 nearly 50,000 full-time teachers – 20,000 more than there had been at the time of the Robbins Report and something like double the number of full-time teachers in the greatly expanded universities. Here was an undertow on all university questions that DES ministers and officials had in future to consider.

Early in 1965 Sir Bruce Fraser ceased to be Joint Permanent Secretary of the bi-focal Department of Education and Science and moved to the recently created Ministry of Land and National Resources. His involvement in the history of the universities was not at an end, but the immediate consequence of his departure was a discontinuance of the joint permanent secretaryship and any attempt at an administrative separation of the kind which the majority of the Robbins Committee had hankered after. Sir Bruce had his part in the felling of the proposed six new universities, the SISTERS and the decision not to amalgamate the colleges of education with the universities. He had little or none in the development of policy that led to the Woolwich speech.

Those parts of the Department that had lived at Richmond Terrace then moved to the main building of the old Ministry of Education in Curzon Street, with its curiously angular rooms, its 'good address' and its remoteness from the general rabbit-warren of Whitehall; and the whole corps of the DES was united under a single Permanent Secretary, Sir Herbert Andrew. Almost at the moment when higher education was riven into two 'sectors' the arrangement offered in recognition of Robbins's hope for a separate Ministry of Higher Education was brought silently to an end.

VII

The System

The creation of the Department of Education and Science, first bi-focal, then single, much lengthened the line of decision between the universities and the Government, and left more room for uncertainty and misunderstanding to develop.

From the university the line ran to the UGC. On a matter affecting universities as a whole it ran thence to the departmental branch (at first UF and G[1] and later HFE 4[2]) concerned with universities. That branch, however, in accordance with universal Whitehall practice, was not permitted to communicate directly with the Treasury: all such communication must be through the departmental Finance Branch. The same applied to Government policy affecting the universities, which had to bounce up and down or among these four steps.

The point of balance, however, remained with the University Grants Committee, and most of this chapter is devoted to describing it as it was at that time and for a considerable number of years afterwards.

The constitutional position of the UGC is not especially clever or unusual. It is simply a committee appointed by the Government, as part of its own organisation, to assess and advise on the distribution of funds for a certain purpose. Other examples are the Royal Commission on Historical Manuscripts, the Royal Commission on Historical Monuments and the Royal Fine Arts Commission. It is not a quango. It has no bank account. No grant is made to it. It has no income or revenue-producing capacity. Its staff is provided by the civil service.

At the time of which I speak the UGC had just moved to its present home at 14 Park Crescent, whose stately façade conceals offices designed to severely economical standards. The UGC carried forward from its Treasury ancestry a combination of grandeur and austerity. It was never shabby or ungenteel, but any hint of lavishness was avoided: so was any impression that it was a Government department.

In any organisation the chief manager must be the most senior figure who is continuously present, and in the early days of the UGC, when

---

[1] Universities, Finance and General.
[2] Higher and Further Education 4. The other three were concerned with other aspects of the subject, including polytechnics.

the chairmanship was part-time, the Chairman played little part in management. Sir Keith Murray, however, was full-time and his ten years of chairmanship had established the Chairman as the principal figure not only in the Committee but in the office. The Chairman thus, in civil service terms, combined the functions of Minister and Permanent Secretary, being enlarged for the first role by the Committee and for the second by the secretariat.

The membership (excluding the Chairman) was nineteen, of whom fourteen were academics currently holding university posts. The minority of five was not, however, insignificant.[3] In a way they represented the pre-1946 tradition of total detachment, and their presence made for balance in discussion. The change in 1946 to a predominantly academic membership was associated with the amendment in the Committee's terms of reference which for the first time introduced national needs as the basis for its discharge of its responsibilities.

Various conventions came over the years to be applied to membership of the Committee: a retiring age of seventy, which is the highest now allowed for a professor by any university; resignation on accepting a vice-chancellorship; a ban on any intervention by a member relating to his or her own university; total confidentiality about the Committee's deliberations. Such conventions (except, perhaps, the last) would have been superfluous for the UGC as it was before 1946, but they were essential for a committee which consisted largely of working academics.

During the period covered by this book the burden carried by membership of the Committee was heavy, and grew heavier. It met[4] ten times a year, on the third Thursday of every month except August and September, each meeting occupying the better part of a working day, and carrying a batch of papers that ran to between fifty and a hundred sheets of foolscap. To these largely executive meetings, at which the Committee reached or approved decisions, Sir John Wolfenden added considerable further responsibilities: a two-day residential autumn meeting (normally held at the Chairman's native university) to consider broader issues and longer perspectives; and the network of sub-committees on the various subject groups, each with its own programme of meetings and visits. Superimposed on all this was the continued practice of visitation by the main Committee.

[3] By convention two of them were always drawn from the schools, and one from the world of business.

[4] I use the past tense in the following descriptive passage about the Committee as I knew it; but I have no reason to think any of it is not substantially valid of the Committee today.

The programme of visitations had enormously increased in comparison with the days before Robbins, let alone those before the War. There were now nearly eighty institutions to be visited, for each component of the Universities of London and Wales was visited separately, and Northern Ireland was now included.[5] This involved the whole Committee, with one or two members of its secretariat – a total of some twenty persons – travelling together on a series of circuits which were usually planned to cover several institutions and therefore lasted for the better part of a week. This travelling in company did more than anything else to sustain the essentially collegiate character of the Committee to which I have already referred, so as to make it almost unique among public bodies. In all the members of the Committee spent thirty or more days of most years in one another's company in meetings or visitations, and if one adds to this the time spent on sub-committees (of which most members had at least one) and reading the voluminous papers, the commitment was about an eighth of working time. The remuneration was modest.[6]

The usual length of a visitation, from the arrival of the Committee to its departure, was twenty-four hours,[7] during which six meetings would take place and, normally, two meals. The papers (apart from an initial brief I shall refer to later) and the attendance on the university side were a matter for the institution visited, but had to follow a prescribed pattern. The first meeting introduced the Vice-Chancellor and his principal academic and administrative colleagues; and the last was with the governing body. At the last meeting, which was preceded by a consultation by the Committee in private, the chief business was a report delivered by the Committee's Chairman describing their experiences and impressions in the course of the day: at one time this address was known as 'the allocution', but the term has fallen into disuse. Sometimes it contained specific decisions, hints of direction, notes of praise or criticism. The fact that it was delivered face to face gave it considerable psychological force, following, as it did, on a tense and exhausting day. The university was allowed to take such notes as it chose, but the Committee's Secretary invariably produced an official record of what the Chairman had said, which was transmitted

---

[5] In the case of London University the main Committee did not visit the medical schools. This was left to the Medical Sub-Committee. The colleges of Oxford and Cambridge, having no financial relationship with the Committee, were not visited.

[6] In 1973 it was £750 a year.

[7] Thirty-six hours at Oxford and Cambridge; twelve for the Senate Institutes of the University of London.

81

to the Vice-Chancellor. It lay with him to decide on its further circulation, but there has been a steady tendency towards a wider distribution.

The four intervening meetings were devoted to the staff and the students, and their composition varied except that one was always with the officers and representatives of the student union. A very common pattern for the other three was the professoriate (or the senate), the junior academic staff and the representatives of the supporting staff – administrative, technical and welfare. This was often valuable and revealing, since it threw up unexpected aspects of the life of the university when the preoccupations of the accommodation officer, the medical adviser, the technicians' branch secretary and student counsellor emerged side by side.

Many attempts were made – it is a question I discuss elsewhere – to persuade the Committee to include in their visitation programme meetings with unions and associations as such. This was invariably declined as an intervention in the normal negotiating position of the university as employer and its organised employees. I am sure that unions and associations played a considerable part in a university's arrangements for receiving the Committee, and such matters as promotion prospects, teaching loads, facilities for research, and the position of staff facing the prospect of change or institutional merger were freely discussable with the Committee: but on no occasion would the Committee act as a formal arbiter or court of appeal on a matter which was properly the subject of internal university negotiation.

The visitation system has been criticised as formal and superficial, and certainly some degree of formality was needed to get as much work done as possible in the time. The accusation of superficiality would have more force if the Committee had not possessed and studied a great deal of information about the university before arriving.

I think it is fair to say that by 1970 the UGC had better, more recent and more readily accessible information about the institutions for which it was responsible than any other governmental organisation. The state of a university's capital programme, its staff–student ratios in each department, the pressure (or lack of it) for admission in different subjects, the number of students living at home, in lodgings and in university residence could, by 1970, be produced very quickly indeed and incorporated in briefs. The time allowed for a visitation was therefore not occupied with random questioning, but was approached with a plan of campaign on the Committee's side, as well as the university's.

The Committee's regular, or business, meetings imposed a more emphatic rhythm on its office than is found in ordinary Government departments, since every financial decision or formal communication with the universities had to receive the approval of the Committee itself. The official of the secretariat responsible for each particular piece of business attended the Committee to explain it and, not infrequently, to take it away for amendment after discussion. This regular, orderly contact between the Committee and its secretariat was very important in establishing mutual confidence.

Committee meetings (but not visitations) were also attended by 'assessors' from the research councils (usually their Chairmen) and the Educational Departments (usually their Permanent Secretaries). This practice went back a long way into the past, and produced a curious problem that illustrates the delicate line the UGC has to tread in its relations with the rest of Whitehall.

The old Ministry of Education had always sent an assessor to UGC meetings and therefore received the papers for them; and this practice continued during the bi-focal period of the DES (1964–5) in relation to the Permanent Secretary concerned with the responsibilities of the old Ministry of Education. But it was not extended to the other Permanent Secretary who was now concerned with universities, any more than it had been extended to his predecessors at the Treasury, when they carried the ultimate responsibility for university finance. The reason for what appears a paradox was perfectly simple: it seemed wrong to invite a representative of the Department being advised to meetings at which that advice was being generated, especially if that Department's interest was solely financial.

But when the bi-focal period came to an end, and the DES could boast only one Permanent Secretary (the one who had always received the Committee's papers in the past) a choice had to be made between two equally well-tried and respectable practices. It would have been nonsensical to start withholding papers bearing on educational policy from the Department concerned with the schools, the training of teachers and the further education provided by local authorities just because it now happened to be responsible financially for universities as well. The papers continued to be sent.

The consequences of this little incident should not be exaggerated: it is only a token of an underlying dilemma. The Committee could, and quite often did, meet without the assessors (or indeed its own officials, with the exception of the Secretary) and withhold the relevant papers from them. Assessors were never present at the autumn meetings on broad policy issues. And they had no part in preparing the advice which the Committee itself received from its officials.

The secretariat of the UGC during what might be called the Augustan period marked by Sir John Wolfenden's chairmanship numbered, altogether, rather more than a hundred. Of these ten were architects and quantity surveyors concerned with the huge building programme, and eighteen were at comparative senior levels of administration: not, perhaps, a large staff for planning and controlling a massive development programme with more than forty independent institutions, but very much larger than it had been when the Robbins Committee was constituted.[8] The universities were now grouped geographically for purposes of capital control. With the larger number of institutions, and the vastly larger sums involved, procedures became more elaborate and complicated, with discretion and informality reduced by precedent.

Nevertheless the principle by which each institution's share of the recurrent grant was placed at the recipient institution's unfettered disposal – the so-called 'block grant principle' – was faithfully maintained. Indeed, the more complex the system as a whole became, and the greater the interest shown by Parliament and public in it, the more dangerous was any breach in the block-grant principle. By agreeing to allocate particular parts of the recurrent grant to particular developments or particular subjects ('ear-marking') the Committee would run the risk of starting an avalanche of competing interests and new responsibilities which it was not equipped to deal with. What is more, it would have moved the Committee's whole operation from the level of dealing with institutions to that of dealing with interests organised across institutions. And the autonomy of the universities themselves would have been destroyed simultaneously from without and from within.[9]

[8] In 1953 the staff of the Committee was twenty-three, which by the date of the Robbins Report had risen to fifty. By 1966 it stood at 116.
[9] The only exceptions were (1) cases where an independent national inquiry had not only established a special need but secured additional funds to meet them – e.g. the grants for Oriental, African and Latin American studies; and (2) cases where a university was acquiring a totally new block of work such as a new medical school or a neighbouring college of education. Even in these cases the UGC put the earliest possible time-limit on the ear-marking it was prepared to allow. The only instance I can recall of the UGC departing from this framework was the allocation to certain extended courses in engineering and technology in 1976–7. The allocation for research in the humanities at about the same time was not made to universities but to the British Academy. The 'New Blood' Scheme falls outside the period of this book, and is a form of ear-marking, but can be justified on the ground that additional funds were made available for it and nothing else.

When the UGC came to distribute block grant, what principles did it follow? Many have sought, and some Cagliostros profess to have found, a formula, a 'black box', but no such formula either existed or could have existed in the changing situation with which the UGC was confronted during those years. On major distributions, such as a quinquennial settlement, the stated needs of each university were the guide, and since these consisted mainly of the cost of existing commitment enhanced by plans for expansion on which the UGC had been previously consulted, this was not very difficult, but the result tended to freeze the pattern. As the distributions become more frequent in the effort to compete with inflation and the sums less adequate, the Committee began to consider successions of hypothetical distributions incorporating various factors before reaching judgments which did not correspond, in particular cases, with any of the formulae. At no period in my experience did the Committee adopt an overriding formula for the distribution of its grant.

The results of insisting on dealing with institutions, not subjects, were in practice much modified from 1964 onwards by the changed balance of grant list, whereby a quarter of its members were institutions concentrating on science and technology.[10] And two others were business schools. The UGC was well aware of the more highly specialised parts of universities, including institutes of London University, and was conscious of the need to protect them. But there was another aspect to this concern, on which the UGC embarked with some reluctance. As early as 1965 it began to consider whether the need for graduates in agriculture justified the existing twelve departments of agriculture; and reached the conclusion that seven would do. This step in the outfield of academic life was more significant than it appeared at the time. The obverse of ensuring that all necessary subjects were cultivated was that some might be over-cultivated, or concentrated at fewer, stronger places. Such steps were few and cautious, but they occurred. Usually they were preceded by an inquiry conducted by an *ad hoc* panel, though sometimes by an appropriate sub-committee of the UGC itself: in either case independent experts from outside the UGC were brought in. Such exercises were valuable, but became increasingly difficult because they had to be confined to institutions on the UGC grant list. In other words the absurdity of trying to guide what was now

[10] The nine former CATs; Imperial College, UMIST, Strathclyde and Heriot Watt — thirteen out of fifty-one.

only part of the system became increasingly apparent. What was the use of seeking to concentrate or rationalise a field of study in the university system if relevant developments were occurring in a rapidly growing 'public sector' to which one's terms of reference did not extend?

These developments inevitably strengthened the long-urged case for parliamentary audit of the university grant and access to all transactions concerned with it by Parliament's servant, the Comptroller and Auditor General; though, by a paradox, the growing 'public sector' was exposed to no such pressure, because it was mainly administered by local authorities. Thus the arrival of parliamentary audit of the university grant meant that the so-called 'independent' sector became subject to far more searching scrutiny from the centre than the sector labelled 'public' and 'responsive' by the Woolwich speech.

As I have said earlier, the immunity of the UGC and the universities from this scrutiny originated at a time when public funds provided less than half the support of universities, and capital grants were rare. Its survival into a period of major capital programmes and escalating recurrent grants had brought increasing pressure from the Public Accounts Committee for the immunity to be removed, and during the 1950's the Treasury, while not yielding the principle, had made certain concessions, notably on capital control. They had stimulated the UGC to appoint inquiries, first under Sir George Gater, then under Sir Arthur Rucker,[11] whose published reports set out the principles on which capital control was to be exercised. The Robbins Committee had argued eloquently that the surviving immunity was an important guarantee of academic freedom, and should be preserved. But when, in 1965, the Public Accounts Committee again demanded full access to both the UGC and the universities, the walls of Jericho fell.

It is not difficult to see why. There could be no convincing answer to the question, 'If you have nothing to hide, why should you object?' The sums of money were enormous, the national importance of the universities undeniable – least of all by the universities themselves. Moreover the arguments on which the Robbins Report had defended the immunity were too sweeping and in at least one respect were based on a mistaken view about the role of the Public Accounts Committee and the Comptroller and Auditor General, which is, by retrospective inquiry, to expose and criticise what they claim to be wasteful or inef-

---

[11] *Methods used by the Universities of Contracting and of Recording and Controlling Expenditure*, Cmnd 9, HMSO, 1956 (Gater), and Cmnd 1235, HMSO 1960 (Rucker). The two papers have the same title.

ficient. Policy decisions maturely, and executive decisions lawfully, arrived at are not for them to question. They thus claim to represent no threat of political intervention.

The true objection to ending the immunity was different, and not an easy one to argue. The fear of being pilloried for a mistake makes for caution, deliberation and unadventurous bureaucracy. After a time so many stable doors may get shut that it becomes almost impossible to move the horses; so many promises are given that this or that shall not be allowed to happen again that it becomes difficult for anything to happen at all; safeguards and the staff to man them multiply, and initiative goes to a discount; and every now and then a manifestly desirable and sensible course of action is abandoned either because there is an element of risk in it or because it offends against some undertaking given in a different context. Such considerations weighed heavily not only with the Treasury when it was responsible, but with the DES Accounting Officers who followed and saw an uncomfortable extension of the area for which they could be personally held accountable, and about which they could receive bleak letters from the Comptroller and Auditor General ending with a valedictory 'yours ever' that had so much more in it of the sinister than of the friendly.

By a great piece of good fortune the Comptroller and Auditor General of the day was an official who well understood the universities and had, in his Treasury days, put the case for their immunity from parliamentary audit. This was Sir Bruce Fraser, who had recently succeeded Sir Edmund Compton. He introduced himself and his audit to the universities with sensitiveness and tact, and although, over the years that followed, some instances of defective judgment and wasteful expenditure have been brought to light (how could it be otherwise?) the universities have on the whole stood up well to scrutiny, and have even received advice which has saved them money. The principle of the block grant has not been eroded, academic decisions have not been questioned.

Just the same, the admission of the Comptroller and Auditor General to the financial business of universities has nudged the whole system further in the direction of Whitehall, and has been felt especially in the University Grants Committee itself, with the results on administration that I have described. If some flaw was found in the building arrangements of a university, how was it that the Committee had not prevented it? Such questions damaged one of the Committee's most precious claims – that it did not run the universities, since they ran themselves; but could it, even if it had wanted to, stand aside and let the unfortunate university take all the blame? Still worse was a growing interest on the part of the Public Accounts Committee about the way the Committee built up its financial advice to the Government. How did it cost developments? Such questions invite the substitution of formulae for judgment, and judgment has always been the raison d'être of the Committee.

The Robbins Report, however, depicts the UGC not only as possessing a raison d'être but as enshrining a principle – the principle of non-interference by Government in the affairs of universities;[12] and it has been said increasingly in recent years that this principle has been undermined. This book certainly shows considerable changes over twenty years in the way universities are financed, a path from comparative affluence to serious, even in some instances crippling, shortage of money, and an uncertain future in which to plan. Has the UGC principle therefore failed?

In two areas to which the Robbins Report attached importance it cannot be said that the principle has in any way been eroded. Not only has the UGC never lent itself to direct political intervention by Government in decisions which lie with universities: it has stood as a barrier against any such ill-judged attempts. Nor has its advice on the distribution of grant between institutions ever been overruled or even questioned by Government.

The source of the criticism lies elsewhere. The system was designed for a world in which the resources devoted to universities either remained level or increased, and not for one in which they contracted. As the Robbins Report itself says:

Needs may be assessed in absolute terms by the University Grants Committee. But their assessment of their importance in comparison with that of other objectives of expenditure must be done by ministers, just as ministers cannot escape a concern for the extent of the total provision for higher education and its broad division between different types of institution.[13]

In short, the UGC may not get all it asks for, and for a long time past this has in fact been the case. When the gap between what the UGC asks for and what Ministers will concede is such that some actual *reduction* in activity is required – a state of affairs which neither the founders of the system nor the Robbins Committee contemplated – severe strains at once develop, since the UGC is faced with the unappe-

---

[12] Paragraphs 725–32.   [13] Paragraph 731.

tising choice of either making the necessary painful decisions itself (and so appearing more interventionist than it should be), or throwing in the sponge altogether and leaving the institutions to cut themselves (in which case it will rightly be accused of abdicating its responsibilities). Whichever course is chosen, the confidence on which the system rests will be diminished, and a profound conflict will develop between the Committee's two principal functions of advising on total needs for what it judges to be a healthy university system and distributing grants to the various institutions. At worst the first of these functions will atrophy, and the initiative on the assessment of need will pass out of the Committee's control altogether into the hands of the Government.

In conditions of contraction the same difficulties will be felt in the autonomous institutions themselves. If the UGC, acting on its judgment, spreads its inadequate resources unevenly, very heavy strains will be imposed on some institutions. If the UGC throws in the sponge the strain will be more widespread but irrational when related to the system as a whole – e.g. a series of unrelated local decisions could cause a particular subject to vanish completely, or remain over-provided. In either case the tension between the management of the university responsible for the institution as a whole, and its component parts, will grow more severe, and corporate spirit will suffer.

In concluding this portrait of the UGC I must mention one other feature of its relationship with the Government, namely its confidentiality. It would be wrong to say that the advice of the Committee has never been officially revealed. Ministers have said from time to time that this or that decision has been taken after consultation with, or even on the advice of, the UGC. The actual distribution of grant by the Committee is, technically speaking, 'advice', and the fact that the Committee has in fact advised on a matter is often reported in its own surveys, together with the outcome. Nevertheless it has always been held that the terms in which the Committee gives its advice must be confidential, in much the same way as the advice of officials to Ministers is confidential. If, it is argued, the Committee's advice was constantly rejected or modified in public its value as an advocate of the universities would be impaired and it would lose the confidence of both the parties between whom it mediates. Its credibility therefore depends very much on the conviction that in any given set of circumstances it will make the best case it can for the universities, and distribute the results with well-informed impartiality. Even the author of Section 2 of Appendix

Four of the Robbins Report, which describes the whole system as it then was in accurate detail, is careful to claim no more.[14]

At the zenith of what I have called the Augustan Age of the universities – which might be put at 1967 – the totality of the administrative apparatus concerned with the programme was very large indeed – much larger than is generally realised. The staff of the UGC, as I have said, more than quadrupled in five years; the new structure of sub-committees – which proved to be one of the most valuable innovations of the Wolfenden period – brought something like 150 people, mostly working academics, into the planning process in addition to the twenty regular members of the main Committee. Essential new parts of the system, though not part of either the UGC or the DES, were the Central Council for Admissions (UCCA) and its godchild the University Statistical Record (USR). The office of the Committee of Vice-Chancellors and Principals (CVCP) was very much enlarged, especially to deal with salary questions. At the DES one entire branch of perhaps thirty persons was concerned exclusively with university and student questions. The arrival of the Comptroller and Auditor General on the scene deployed some fifteen auditors. But most numerous of all were the additions to the administrative staffs of the universities themselves. The handling of their building projects, the administration of their students and academic staff, their enormously increased relations with other authorities, their involvement in trade union negotiations, health, safety, fire, public relations, produced a university bureaucracy on a scale never previously experienced, and not emotionally allowed for. It was unexpected, yet inevitable, and contributed to the change in the picture that coincides with the ending of the sixties. Altogether – though it is no more than a guess – the administration of the programme engaged not less than 5,000 people in one way or another; and this is without counting those working on research into higher education and on *The Times Higher Educational Supplement*. In short, the late sixties saw

[14] 'In advising on the overall level of building starts, the Committee is advisory in the strictest sense. Its advice is not made public, and subsequent discussions with the Committee are confidential. The final decision on the overall size of the building programme is made by the Government' (paragraph 35). 'When the UGC's Quinquennial Report has been considered, a decision on the total amount of the recurrent grant is made by the Government' (paragraph 45). 'These arrangements retain to the Government responsibility for the overall level of recurrent and non-recurrent grants; and thus a determining influence on the overall size of university development. They also allow the Government, in certain respects, and in accordance with academic advice, to influence the direction of development' (paragraph 57). It was plainly axiomatic to the writer that there would always be some measure of development.

the creation of an administrative, semi-political, and so abrasive collectivity, which had not existed before and which would have been unrecognisable to those who had projected the University Grants Committee.

VIII

High Noon

The system just described reached its apogee, and the tide of university growth advanced more rapidly than at any time in this century, during the period from 1965 to 1968 when Anthony Crosland was Secretary of State. The quinquennial grant of 1962 had originally been set (after a desperate struggle) at £56m – later raised to £61m in the light of Robbins. That of 1967 envisaged a growth to £172.5m by 1972 – almost a threefold increase in a period of mild inflation derived from the experience of the first half of the decade. In the same period of two quinquennia it was planned that the number of university students should double from 113,000 in 1962 to 225,000 in 1972. By 1967 the number of postgraduates was far outrunning the projections of the Robbins Report, generous though these had seemed. The neglect of medical studies was repaired by plans to raise the annual entry from the 1961 level of about 2,000 to 3,000,[1] and by 1966 no fewer than fifteen universities were bidding for new medical schools. Staffing ratios were more than maintained. Already, as the new buildings approved since 1959 came into use, university precincts all over Britain were being transformed.[2]

Crosland was particularly well suited for this sanguine, expansive time. Large, genial, highly intelligent, instinctively moderate, decisive, the brightest star of the Oxford PPE School, he was a child of the age. He enjoyed exercising power, and perhaps thought its limits were less narrow than in fact they were in an educational system where self-government was deeply entrenched on every side. The touches of arrogance and doctrinaire feeling which he displayed – the arrogance was part of his character – in no way affected the generosity with which he handled the higher education programme. As an education Minister he may have been less sensitive than Boyle, less dramatic than Hailsham, but with the exception of Mrs Thatcher he towers above all his successors in that office during the period covered by this book.

[1] For some reason the size of medical education is always measured by entries, not by total numbers. Troy weight as against avoirdupois.
[2] New building started between 1959 and 1969 with UGC funds had a face value of about £300m including site costs (but not including equipment and furniture). The equivalent today would be about £2 billion.

He was a convivial man, and not given to lonely decision. Still less
was he a rubber stamp for official proposals. He was far more venture-
some than the cautious and non-interventionist Sir Herbert Andrew,
who was Permanent Secretary throughout his time. He had an informal
coterie for the discussion of education policy which met regularly in
his house at Holland Park, with a standing membership of Labour
sympathisers drawn from the educational world, to which senior civil
servants were occasionally asked. There he would buoyantly bathe in
opinions and reach resolutions – among them the resolution that no
further institutions of higher education could be wrested from local
authority control.

Crosland, perhaps, never saw the deeper implications of dividing
higher education into two segments with different autonomous systems:
he was far too much of an Oxonian to regard the universities with
the same kind of disapproval as he felt for the public schools. The
polytechnic policy, so far as he was concerned, was a response to a
far narrower political imperative – the impossibility, as he saw it, of
a Labour Secretary of State taking institutions from urban local education authorities which were predominantly controlled by Labour, and
bringing them under the same regime as the universities.

In no sense did this mean he was averse from the Grants Committee
principle so far as the universities were concerned. It seemed to him
right, and he well understood the protection it gave him from detailed
and thorny responsibilities. Attempts were naturally made by his
university friends to enlist his influence in this or that university struggle, but they were genially shrugged off. In this he was much assisted
by the fact that the times were especially propitious to the exercise
of real power by the University Grants Committee, freshly gilded by
the enthusiastic phraseology of the Robbins Report.

Control of the building programme was what conferred real authority
on the University Grants Committee during these years. Recurrent
grant required judgment at the margins and was distributed to the
universities with advice, admonition and diplomacy – but the money
once given was at the disposal of the university to which it was awarded.
It was through the decisions on buildings that the Committee exerted
direct and specific power over each university and the system as a
whole. It is true that even building proposals originated with individual
universities, and once a project was approved it was for the university
to handle the contract – an arrangement which undoubtedly made the
work move vigorously ahead; but it was for the UGC alone to decide

which proposals to select in the light of its general overview and its particular opinion of the university concerned, and to fix limits of cost within which each should be built. With the decline of the university building programme in the seventies the UGC was bound to appear as depending more on consultation and persuasion, and less on direct power. During the sixties, however, with the control of massive capital, UGC executive power in relation to both the universities and the Government was at its highest.

And on the whole the university capital programme was one of the most successful in that building-dominated decade. Serious delays in buildings coming into use were few, and considering the scale of operations the proportion of actual mishaps was very low indeed.[3] Some of the officials groaned about the proclivities of some universities to appoint prestigious and therefore, they suspected, expensive architects, but the business of extracting value for money was pressed vigorously forward, as it had been earlier in the simpler field of school building. Adaptation of the building systems developed for schools was less straightforward than the enthusiasts for them had hoped, given the greater complexity of university buildings and the higher sophistication of those who were to use them, but even here there were successes, of which the University of Bath is a notable monument. The information on which the UGC reached its decisions steadily improved, as did the procedures for examining applications.

The power of the UGC exercised through the capital programme, though great, was subject to a severe constraint imposed by past decisions about the pattern of institutions. Those which were to be developed on new sites – the eight new universities and the CATs that moved – had to be built up to a viable size if money already committed was not to go waste. So out of a total of £152m allocated to university buildings for the years 1965 to 1969 inclusive, more than one-third – £57m – went to those ten institutions, though they contributed nothing like a third of the extra students proposed for the early seven-

[3] The collapse of a building under construction in Aberdeen in freak weather conditions caused loss of life. Unforeseeable subsidence led to the later loss of a building at the University of Kent. Insufficiently tested innovations in technique (such as the use of high-alumina cement, common in the sixties) caused some subsequent trouble and expense; and may yet cause more. The building programme was pressed forward with the utmost urgency, and prefabricated building methods then in vogue were widely and enthusiastically used. Those who now criticise the results on aesthetic grounds should remember the impatience of the public demand for immediate expansion and the rejection of any idea (which was canvassed rather hopelessly by the Treasury) that part of it should be met initially by temporary structures.

ties. It was well that in the autumn of 1964 the decision had been taken to bury the Robbins recommendations for even more new institutions. Even so the UGC had little money left to deal with the more decrepit and inefficient buildings in the older universities, large numbers of which were carried forward into the seventies and eighties.

The University Estate which was created out of grant had (and has) a peculiar status for which it is difficult to find a parallel in modern Government finance. Since universities were not governmental institutions, the buildings were not owned by the Government; and since, unlike local authorities, universities did not possess statutory powers to raise revenue from which loan charges could be met, additions to the Estate provided by grant simply became the property of the university concerned.[4] The alternative of raising loan charges and then meeting them by an addition to the recurrent grant would have seemed absurdly elaborate, but the fact remains that the annual costs always omitted much of the element for rent, and this makes comparisons with the annual cost of local authority institutions difficult. The practice, simple though it seemed, also stored up a certain amount of tension for the future. Such huge assets, created by public funds for specific public purposes, could hardly be allowed to be diverted from those purposes without some kind of safeguard: suppose a university, having obtained a building on grounds of high academic priority, then sold it and used the proceeds to fund an activity which the UGC would not have supported if it had been asked directly? For this reason the apparently generous freeholds had a conditional element. If they were sold the proceeds had to be returned to the Exchequer. The UGC could not dispense with this rule, nor did its programme receive any addition as a result of such 'surrenders'. Naturally, therefore, such sales rarely occurred, even when, owing to changes of plan, a building or a site was no longer needed.

The 1960s were also the golden age of the quinquennial system of recurrent grant; and its resilience surprised even some of those who

[4] An exception must be made in respect of the schemes for student residence built by loan, which began in the late sixties. Here, of course, revenue from rents paid by the occupants was supposed to cover the loan charges. But in this case too the cost of the loan charges was largely met from another pocket of public funds, since most of the occupants received grants. As interest rates soared with inflation demands were naturally made for either an increase in the rate of student grant or a level of rent which would have had to be subsidised from recurrent grant designed for other purposes. This latter the UGC naturally and firmly refused to allow. The pressure on the student support system was therefore severe.

were most enthusiastically committed to it. So great was this confidence that as the 1962–7 quinquennium neared its end it became possible to introduce an even greater degree of financial continuity in an effort to meet the one objection the universities still had to the traditional system. As one quinquennium drew to a close the uncertainty about the pitch of the next caused unease in the universities, even though there was at that time an implicit undertaking that its first year would at any rate not fall below the last year of its predecessor. But in 1966 the DES and the Treasury agreed to give a provisional minimum for 1967 before the 1967–72 quinquennium had been settled, and that it would be at least a bit higher.[5]

Several other moves were made towards a more generous and flexible financial regime. The old rule by which equipment attracted grant only if it was needed for new buildings was replaced by a regular block grant for equipment which each university could use (and indeed accumulate) at its discretion. The Flowers Report established in the Computer Board a large new source of funds by which a university-based network of computer facilities came rapidly into existence.[6] The ratio of senior to junior posts was improved.[7] Altogether, then, the picture on the surface could hardly have seemed happier for the universities than it did in the academic year 1967–8 – the third of Anthony Crosland's tenure as Secretary of State and the fourth of Sir John Wolfenden's chairmanship of the UGC. Capital programmes had been announced for four years ahead. The recurrent grant statement for the next quinquennium took the settlement on an ascending scale to 1971–2. The initial numbers proposed in the Robbins short-term programme were certain to be achieved, and a longer-term target that

---

[5] The 'provisional year', as it was called, was announced in December 1966 for the academic year beginning in August 1967, and was £147.5m: £8.5m more than 1966–7. Even this, however, did not fully satisfy those in the universities who sought certainty and pressed for a series of overlapping settlements ('rolling quinquennia') that would give a perpetual horizon of at least three years. But this was rejected as likely to impose an impossible burden on the system.

[6] *Council for Scientific Policy and University Grants Committee Joint Working Party on Computers in Research*, Cmnd 2883, HMSO, 1966. This ended the unsatisfactory arrangement by which university computers were settled by an *ad hoc* UGC Panel. While the Panel did good work it had to compete for funds within the UGC structure, and lacked the effective power to ear-mark grant for the recurrent cost of computer installations. The rapidity with which computer technology was developing, the need for it to be nationally planned, and the issues arising from the policy of protecting the British computer industry were best dealt with by a separate authority with new funds.

[7] Professorships were brought into the reckoning of senior posts, but the proportion of senior to junior posts was adjusted so as more than to compensate for this change.

was still higher had been set up, together with recurrent finance which implied little if any diminution in the average cost per student.[8]

Yet underneath this smiling surface the atmosphere was already becoming unhealthy, and there were a number of signs that all was not well. The universities were too much in the public eye. Until 1960 I do not suppose that there was a single ministerial utterance in Parliament about the universities except at the long intervals when statements about grant were made or the House of Lords devoted an evening to well-informed but unexciting discussion of the subject. The impact of the Robbins Report had changed all that. The universities had become a major public programme, and so were inevitably caught in any eddy set up by the sporadic attempts at the centre to bring public expenditure under control. Announcements affecting them were therefore becoming frequent and sudden, in a shape which was often dictated by a pattern arrived at centrally and designed to save money in the shorter term. Little time was allowed to study and work out the consequences of these central decisions.

The first of this long series was the Chancellor of the Exchequer's announcement as early as 27 July 1965 that a substantial amount of university (and other) building planned to start in the current year would be 'deferred'. Since expenditure on a major building project in its first year is only about 10 per cent of its total cost, a very large number of starts have to be 'deferred' to make up an appreciable saving in the short term: in fact nearly half the building due to be started in 1965–6 was 'deferred' in order to save the relatively small sum of £1.5m, and since a good deal of it had already started, almost all the rest – however needful – had to be stopped.

I have put quotation marks round the word 'defer' because it contained an element of humbug. In practice 'deferment' meant permanent loss to the programme – not indeed of the actual buildings 'deferred' but of those which they displaced a year or two later.[9] 'Deferment' was to be inflicted twice more, in January, and again in July, 1968, and resulted in the loss of some 20 per cent of the programmes for 1967–8, 1968–9 and 1969–70. By the last of these years expenditure on universities had in any case begun to lose its political attractiveness

---

[8] The average recurrent grant per student in 1962 was £550. That planned for 1971–2 (at 1966 prices) was £782. During the period 1962 to 1966 inflation was about 5 per cent per annum.

[9] On this first occasion the position was largely restored by the announcement of December 1965, which raised the starts for the two succeeding years by £12m. Even so the programme permanently lost £3m.

for reasons to be examined later. These upsets do not detract from the general success of the programme, but they did unfavourably affect its balance, since it was natural, when these sudden storms blew, to exercise such choice as there was in favour of new and urgent buildings. Replacement and extension were the usual victims of 'deferment', and the tendency to neglect obsolescence was reinforced as a result.

An equally serious and more lasting malaise was developing over the question of academic salaries – one that it is not too much to say has been pursued almost from its beginning by the Eumenides, cursed by the Stroke Dolorous, and subject to malign influences from Outer Space.

Here, too, the concerns of central Government about broader questions which had little or nothing to do with universities were an important cause of difficulty. By the early sixties the level of rewards for particular groups in society had become a national and political preoccupation. Within Government, by a series of decisions with which Otto Clarke had had much to do, pay became a separate subject with its own doctrines and methods, which had far more to do with comparison between groups than with the service which each group provided, and were administered by officials who were not primarily concerned with the particular programme to which any particular salariat belonged. Indeed these officials were professionally required to regard their colleagues concerned with particular programmes with some wariness, as likely to advance arguments which did not fit in to whatever 'pay policy' was current. To that extent the demand by the university teachers to 'meet the paymaster' was based on an illusion, for the 'paymaster' with whom they were ultimately confronted was not the Government as the financier of the university programme but the Government with its eye on the whole range of pay settlements, in which the pay of university teachers was a modest, if unduly conspicuous, eminence.

There were, however, other difficulties, which were never openly admitted, though they poisoned many discussions. Since, in the nature of the case, a university system provides for the teaching and study of everything that can reasonably be taught and studied – from Assyriology to solid state physics, from architecture to haematology, from veterinary surgery to Japanese history, one may question whether academics form a coherent group from the point of view of pay policy at all. A very large number of them must, as a condition of their effectiveness as teachers and researchers, also practise as doctors, architects, accountants and similar structured professions to which they not unreasonably expect their reward should, in one way or another, correspond. Others again are in a position to attract substantial consultancy income, say as geologists or computer scientists. Alongside these are a majority for whom the university salary is the staple. Their books and articles form part of their professional output for which most of them get little if any additional financial reward.

Underneath this layer of difficulty lies another, which is even less often stated. The specific obligations of a university teacher when set out to someone who thinks of a job as requiring physical attendance more or less during daylight hours for five days a week, and forty-six or more weeks a year, seem modest – indeed bald. Such a person is not satisfied by evidence that many academics are very busy people indeed, devoting more hours to their profession than ordinary office workers. He still suspects that the attraction of being free to do the minimum will not be without its influence on some, and he was duly to be confirmed in this opinion by the appearance of several scathing works of fiction based on university life, such as *The History Man*. The dilution which necessarily accompanied the first great wave of expansion, and the heady novelty of the world in which new recruits at that time found themselves, gave added strength to these undercurrents of doubt.

Yet attempts to define functions more amply for jobs with a large intellectual content are rarely successful, and in the case of university teachers they are self-defeating.[10] There are several reasons for this. One lies in the need to provide in the system for rare specialities, which in their nature will attract few students, but must somewhere be cultivated. Even in large and busy departments the pressure on individuals will vary. These problems can be smoothed by good organisation, but they will always be there, and in the the sixties there was still much to learn about effective organisation. But the most important reason is that the indispensable freedom of the teacher to organise his own time within the general requirement to be present in the university is the essential counterpart of the freedom of the university itself. The only remedy against the persistently ineffective, in universities as elsewhere, is a critical attitude to their retention – not easy, it must be admitted, but easier than trying to define exactly what university teachers should do.

[10] Consider the elaborate attempts made in the contracts originally proposed for teachers in polytechnics.

This congeries of problems was referred in 1965 to the then custodian of incomes policy, the National Incomes Commission, which awarded an additional 5 per cent. Not only did this fall short of what was needed to remove current complaints about comparisons, it did not include the clinical teachers in medical schools, who were required to await the findings of the body then reviewing the salaries of doctors as a whole. That body duly reported in May 1966, and what appeared to be the entirely mechanical process of applying those findings to the medical schools began: but this was still in progress some two months later when, on 20 July 1966, the Prime Minister announced a freeze on all unsettled pay claims. Since the medical teachers were regarded as a separate group their claim was declared to be unsettled (although the main body of doctors had settled theirs, arising from the same award) and they got nothing. This was the third injection of venom into the subject which now acquired the sombre heading 'Dons' Pay' in Whitehall. The overriding impression it left with the victims was that the Government had little sympathy for the university profession.

They can hardly be blamed, though it was not true. Indeed one development of the time was the negotiation of a new pension scheme for university teachers which ranks among the most generous available, and has saved many members of the profession from a poverty-stricken old age as well as relieving the university budget of costs to counter inflation which would, as things turned out, have been crippling. The existing scheme offered the retired academic a lump sum based on his and his university's actual contributions over his working life. The existing pensioners, even if they had invested their lump sums wisely, already needed supplementation from their former employers if they were to survive, and this was an increasing charge on the university grant. This creaking scheme was replaced by one which offered a pension – index-linked – related to the final salary of the individual. The committee which produced this scheme under the chairmanship of the late Sir George Maddex was one of the most gruelling I have ever taken part in, but the great thing about the outcome was that academics achieved a reasonable provision for retirement in an age of inflation and the university grant lost an immeasurable liability, which enabled the UGC to find more money for academic purposes without actually increasing its demands for grant.[11]

[11] Of course the recurrent grant had to bear the cost of the very heavy employers' contribution in the new scheme. But the overall financial effect of funding a huge future liability instead of entrusting it to the vagary of future Exchequer grants has undoubtedly been beneficial.

In comparative silence other trends were making progress which in the end eroded the quinquennial system and undermined the traditional role of the UGC. It will be remembered that by convention quinquennial settlements were revised during their currency on three grounds only: a change of policy in respect of student numbers; an approved change in the pay-scale of *academic* staff; and a sufficiently marked change in the level of non-teaching costs as measured by a special index known, after the economist who devised it, as the 'Brown Index'. Reopening on this third ground, however, could be refused. At best it meant an *ad hoc* exercise in persuasion each time.

During the middle sixties these conventions were on the whole observed; but the last of them was showing signs of strain under the pressure for increases in the pay of the growing number of employees of universities who were not academics. What was happening here was not inflation but relative revaluation of the work they did – a process which was making rapid advances throughout society in the 1960s under the twin influences of unionisation and full employment. The cost of this was an important element in the 'Brown Index'.

From 1964 onwards the unionisation of the non-academic staff spread very quickly indeed, above all among the technical staff of science and engineering departments, under the energetic leadership of the ASTMS. The universities were ill prepared for such a development, and had given little thought to the stony world of industrial relations of the kind professed by Clive Jenkins and, very soon afterwards, by the leaders of the TGWU, NALGO and NUGMW. Even when in 1965 a degree of coordination among the managements began to appear in the shape of what was called at first 'the employers' club' they were placed in the uncomfortable position of negotiating without being quite sure where the money for the settlement was going to come from. In due course more formal arrangements under the aegis of the Committee of Vice-Chancellors and Principals came into existence,[12] but the university negotiators could never be quite sure whether a doleful appeal through the UGC to the Government would be more effective than resolute resistance to the skilful and hardfaced men from the unions.

The story of technicians' salaries needs to be carried a little further

---

[12] The 'employers' club' was succeeded by the more formal University Council for Technical Trades (UCTT) which in turn was replaced (in June 1970) by the technicians' panel of a comprehensive body for negotiating the salaries and conditions of non-teaching staff called the Central Council for Non-Teaching Staffs in Universities.

to illustrate how the recurrent costs of universities were outrunning the estimates made only a few years earlier for the Robbins Committee. In 1968 the unions claimed an increase of 12½ per cent, to which the universities, having been warned there would be no supplementation for this item, replied with an offer of 4½. Industrial action followed – the first time universities had faced such a thing. The shock may have been sharp at that time, but its longer consequences, bringing the whole of the university system within the scope of industrial warfare, were historic.

Inevitably the UGC, though it had neither powers nor money to intervene, was drawn in as a mediator, and a figure of 7 per cent was at last agreed for payment from 1 April 1969. But before that date arrived a further claim was tabled by the unions, this time for 21 per cent, and it was conceded, bringing the increase for some 12,000 technical staff to 28 per cent in a single year. The cost had not been underwritten by any promise of additional grant, and was never fully recovered in supplementation. Nor was this all. By job description, itemisation of duties and complex machinery for grading, the overall remuneration of technicians was increased even more than these figures would suggest. It could be argued that until then the universities had exploited their subordinate staff, but it was not taken into account by the system of support. The index of expenditure per student at constant prices, which had risen steadily until 1968, sank below pre-Robbins levels from 1969 onwards.[13]

These troubles about costs and salaries, which were to become chronic, damaged not only the universities but the UGC and the financial system it represented. When the UGC was drawn, as it increasingly was, into negotiations about salaries, the result was to throw the ambiguity of its position into cruel relief. That ambiguity was well understood and accepted when the UGC was acting as a channel flowing in both directions between university managements and Government; but the UGC had little to offer in a situation where the university world was at odds with itself, and successive crises led to demands for direct access to the ultimate source of funds – the Government. Indeed it was unreasonable to expect a Committee that consisted largely

[13] See *UGC Annual Survey for 1969–70*, Cmnd 4593, HMSO, 1971, Appendix VI. At constant (1967–8) prices expenditure per student rose from £752 in 1959–60 to a peak of £900 in 1966–7 and fell to £864 in 1968–9. An index based on 1957–8 = 100 in the same Appendix shows the peak a little earlier (106.1 in 1964–5) and the drop below 100 (to 98.2) in 1969–70.

of working academics to assume responsibility for academic salaries.[14] The Chairman and officials were uncertain whether their duty lay in supporting the university managements or in arguing for the maximum conservation of resources already destined for the universities.

The problem of negotiating machinery for academic salaries (but not the underlying malaise produced by perpetual salary claims) was resolved by the ingenuity of Sir Toby Weaver, who devised the present system of two negotiating committees, one consisting of representatives of the university managements and the Association of University Teachers under an independent chairman, to agree on proposals they could jointly put forward; and the other, in which Government representatives joined them, for discussion of those proposals directly between the Government and the universities. The UGC had a walking-on part in both scenes of this long-running drama, and behind them could still exert some influence, but the fact of the matter was that from 1968 onwards, when the new system was introduced, the UGC principle ceased to apply to that aspect of university finance. This was the inevitable concomitant of incomes policy and unionisation.

The impact of inflation, the arrival of incomes policy and the rapid advance of unionism among university staff did much to undermine the hopes of the Robbins Committee, but one could hardly expect its Report to have foreseen these developments. The tilting of the balance of studies in favour of science in a period of rapid expansion was, however, one of its principal recommendations, and within about two years the consequences of this were beginning to be noticed in uncomfortable ways.

In accordance with the Robbins Report two-thirds of the very large building programmes for the years 1963 to 1966 were devoted to projects in science and technology. The creation of new departments and the recruitment of new staff had followed the same pattern. Very large sums had been spent on developing the former colleges of advanced technology (now universities) and the three major technological institutions in London, Manchester and Glasgow. In addition, by the end

[14] For a number of years this difficulty had been patched over by adding two non-academic persons of distinction to the Committee 'for salary purposes only'. Their function was, on behalf of the whole Committee, to examine and verify academic salary proposals arrived at within the university system before they were submitted to the Government as recommended. But they were neither negotiators nor arbitrators, and once considerations of incomes policy had begun to enter the scene their usefulness was at the end. I have passed over the weary story of the reference of university pay to the National Board for Prices and Incomes from 1968 to 1970 (NBPI Reports 98 and 145, Cmnd 3866, HMSO, 1968, and Cmnd 3979, HMSO, 1970).

of 1966, the designation of the polytechnics had begun, and this new range of institutions was expected to provide further places in science and technology, especially the latter.

It began to be observed that some of the less prestigious (or well-known) science and engineering departments were finding it difficult to attract as many students as they were designed to take, and that in general lower standards of entry were resulting. The same tendencies began to appear in some science and technology courses at postgraduate level, though in these some of the places that would otherwise have remained empty were taken up by students from overseas. Simultaneously entry into arts and social science faculties was becoming more competitive. The reproachful cry of 'empty places in science and technology' was taken up by the press.

As early as January 1965, the University Central Council for Admissions reported that the universities could have taken 1,500 more students in science and technology 'had suitable candidates presented themselves', and very soon afterwards the newly constituted Council for Scientific Policy (CSP) commissioned an inquiry into the position under the chairmanship of the Vice-Chancellor of Nottingham, Dr (now Sir Frederick) Dainton. It was quickly found that there were no adequate figures for an effective study of what was happening in the schools, where the root of the problem certainly lay,[15] and since these had to be collected specially, detailed findings did not appear until February 1968.[16]

They showed that while the number of children studying science was continuing to grow in the schools, both absolutely and as a proportion of the age group, it was not rising nearly so rapidly as that of children studying other subjects.[17] The outcome showed up only too

---

[15] The absence of meaningful figures on the examination performance of boys and girls when called for by the Dainton inquiry in 1965 shows that they were not available to the Robbins committee three or four years earlier; and that that Committee's hope for a rapid growth in qualified science and technology students was based on fragmentary data, optimistically interpreted.

[16] Cmnd 3451, HMSO, 1968.

[17] The key figures are probably those given in Table 39 of the Report, which show the percentages and numbers of boys and girls securing GCE O-levels or CSE Grade I in science subjects in successive years. In 1952 the proportion was 34 per cent boys and 19 per cent girls; in 1962, 43 per cent boys and 23 per cent girls; and in 1966 42 per cent boys and 22 per cent girls. The actual numbers, of course, had risen considerably between the first and last of these years, though oddly enough the absolute number of girls taking science subjects at that level actually dropped between 1962 and 1966. The whole success of the programme depended on it rising sharply. In 1964–5 (see *Returns from Universities* for that year) there were just over 20,000 students in applied science.

clearly in the admissions for 1966 as compared with those for 1962. Entries in science subjects had gone up by 34 per cent and in technology by 35 per cent against an overall growth of 42 per cent, so arts and social science had gone up by 58 per cent. 'With the continuation of present trends universities will find themselves', the Dainton Committee concluded, 'increasingly recruiting rather than selecting candidates in science and technology. Indeed if present entry requirements are maintained throughout the quinquennium, universities are likely to be faced with a dearth of suitable *candidates* in science and technology, and a shortage of *places* in other subjects.'

The Dainton Report was followed by an immediate reversal of UGC (and Robbins) policy. In their *Survey* for the year 1966–7[18] the UGC reported the quinquennial settlement for 1967 to 1972 (which envisaged a growth in real terms of 15 per cent over the five years and a student target of at least 220,000) and observed that it was apparent from recent studies (such as those conducted by Dr Dainton on behalf of the CSP), that 'the pressure of demand from the schools for places in science and technology could not be expected to increase much, if at all'. The capital programme was adjusted accordingly, but adjusting a capital programme of that size is like swinging an ocean liner through ninety degrees. It takes some time. Many scientific buildings in progress were duly completed; and the polytechnic programme proceeded.

Simultaneously with the inquiry into 'empty places' the Council for Scientific Policy had to take up investigation of another criticism which was ventilated under the cheap but catching phrase of the 'brain drain'. The coarseness of the the phrase was not quite accidental since it brought into the discussion of higher education a jingoist note of a kind which had not been heard before. The cry was that valuable academics – above all scientists – were being lured out of Britain by better salaries and facilities for study. The principal lure was, of course, the United States, where the themes the Robbins Report had developed in Britain were fructifying on a scale which makes the Robbins estimates seem the work of officials with square toes and steel spectacles.

This was the first time in history, I think, at which inhabitants of Britain have been criticised by their fellow-countrymen for seeking their fortunes in the wider world. To come to a more practical point, there was no way of stopping it, and for both these reasons I felt neither

Less than 500 were girls. But there were already nearly as many girls in arts departments as there were boys (24,000).

[18] Cmnd 3510, HMSO, 1968.

sympathy nor power to help. The vague ideas of fining the learned man who took a post abroad, and the futile plan of sending emissaries to appeal to the patriotism of those who had taken foreign posts, were equally ineffective and unappealing. They did not correspond to academic principles, whereby study is valid regardless of geographical location.

The 'brain drain' did, however, impoverish British science at the very time when expansion was diluting its quality. The underlying theme of both inquiries was a creeping sense of uncertainty, of which there had been no signs only a few years earlier, about the social and educational base for scientific advance on the scale proposed. This uncertainty most frequently took the form of calls for 'manpower planning' in one shape or another: but every essay in this direction fell foul of the conceptual difficulty which it had in common with incomes policy – the effectual measures could not be reconciled with the freedom of individuals and groups.

It was not therefore an accident that the first inquest into what was happening to the Robbins expansion was undertaken by the Council for Scientific Policy, and not by the University Grants Committee. The flaw in the Robbins Report had not been in the scale of the expansion it proposed, but in the mismatch between it and the potentialities of a largely unreformed system in the schools and their curriculum. Far from providing larger numbers of sixth-formers with the requisite training and inclination for scientific studies at degree standard, the tendency of the school system was rather (and this was applicable to all faculties – the arts included) to reduce the amount of knowledge expected of university entrants in any one subject.

Just before Christmas 1967, on 21 December, Mr Crosland announced that, while no general increase in university fees was desirable, the grant would take account of an assumed fee income of £250 in respect of each new student from outside the UK who started a course from 1967 onwards. This would apply not only to universities but to equivalent courses in local authority further education. The consequences of this decision were far-reaching.

IX

The Dangers of Money-Go-Rounds

Mr Crosland's announcement on fees and its consequences require discussion of a phenomenon which is not uncommon in Government finance and might be called, for want of a better term, the money-go-round.

A money-go-round consists of the creation of Government money under one heading and simultaneous provision for it to disappear under another heading in the public accounts so as to leave expenditure as a whole more or less the same. The purpose may be to avoid some larger inconsistency, or to produce the appearance that something has been done when in fact nothing has been done, or to provide colour for doing something which, if done directly, would arouse opposition. It usually stimulates additional administrative costs; and even if designed not to produce any overall effect on expenditure may acquire a dynamism of its own. A money-go-round out of control can be very dangerous indeed.

An illustration of a small money-go-round can be found in the device adopted when the Board of Inland Revenue was victorious in a battle to tax a large sum of money paid by a company to one of its directors who normally resided in Canada, but attended occasional meetings of the board in London. This sum, said the company, represented travelling expenses in their service. No, said the Revenue, the cost of travelling to work is not an expense, so what he receives is pay, and therefore taxable. The fact that he lives in Canada and works (among other places) in London is his affair, and nothing to the purpose.

As a result of this case there was an immediate tax liability on travelling expenses paid by the Government itself to people who attended Government committees if they received any payment (however small) for doing so. Thus, if a professor in a Scottish university belonged to a research council in London, half – or more – of his return fare would go in tax, and this might well be more than his daily fee (also taxed). In other words he was considerably out of pocket as a result of being a member of a research council. The solution was to pay such people enough extra travelling money to put them back where they had been before – an extremely time-consuming operation, since each case was different and the extra payments themselves were taxable, so that 'grossing up', as it was known, was rather like running up a moving staircase going downwards. The administrative cost almost certainly exceeded the extra tax collected.

A trivial example. A more striking one, which affected the universities much more directly, concerned the payment of rates by universities. As property owners universities are liable to rates, but for many years down to 1965 they were treated as educational charities – that is to say they were liable only to reduced rates sympathetically imposed by local authorities, which in many cases not only admired their local university but provided it with active financial support. Moreover the extent of university buildings was not in those days enormous, and their valuation for rating purposes presented problems which nobody particularly wanted to argue about. The modest sums levied in this spirit had been added, for many years past, to the annual grant made by the UGC, and were ear-marked for the purpose.

Three developments changed this comfortable scene. The gathering momentum of the building programme from 1960 onwards produced an increasing acreage of buildings in locations all over the country which naturally whetted the appetite of that side of local government which sees rateable value in every square foot of structure. Alongside this was a gradual withering of local authority affection and support for universities, which now seemed to be parts of a national picture and to have a bottomless national Exchequer behind them. Against this the local benefits conferred by a university seem to have counted for little.[1]

The third factor was the advent in the new Labour Government of 1964 of R. H. S. Crossman as Minister of Housing and Local Government. During the earlier part of his political career, when he was still a Fellow of New College, Crossman had been a member of the Oxford City Council and as such had long denounced the loss of income suffered by the authority through the relief given to the university and college buildings which crowded the centre of Oxford. I doubt if he distinguished clearly between the colleges and the university on this question, though their position for rating purposes was quite different.

[1] At the time, it was calculated that the presence of a university brought purchasing power into a locality at the rate of about £1,000 per student. In many cases it provided an art gallery, a museum or a park (perhaps all three) at no cost to the ratepayer. It also offered extramural classes, cultural events and conferences to swell the minds and purses of the inhabitants.

For Crossman, probably, as for most people, the colleges were the university.

However that may be, he came to the Ministry of Housing and Local Government resolved that universities should be fully rated, and was quite undeterred when it was pointed out that if this were done the charge would have to fall on the Exchequer, since the universities would otherwise only be able to pay by diverting money from teaching and research. Perhaps in tougher times advantage would have been taken of Mr Crossman's commitment to make the universities find the cost without increasing the grant. So far as I know it was not even thought of. It would have been an interference with the level of the recent quinquennial settlement designed to set the universities on the Robbins path, and Crossman himself would have shrunk from such a solution. The established tradition was followed. When the universities lost their relief (which it turned out could be done by statutory order), the increased charge was added to the UGC grant. The universities simply sent their rates bills to the UGC who paid them. The colleges of Oxford and Cambridge, not being dependent on the UGC, and possessing a different charitable status, which could not be reached by statutory order, escaped. Everyone was happy. The local authorities rejoiced over their enhanced revenue from rates, and perhaps hardly noticed when it was taken into account by Crossman's department in distributing rate support grant and rate equalisation grant to those which had universities on their territory.

But having clicked into existence the nonsense began gradually to assume a life of its own. After all it was worth several millions a year, or seemed to be: and every year it grew. It was a very good example of its species, an accounting device introduced to meet susceptibilities, not clarify the accounts: and it made it look as if the universities were costing more.[2]

It was not long, therefore, before university rates began to attract the attention of the Committee of Public Accounts, which, it will be

---

[2] In economic terms, of course, it has a meaning as the cost of local authority services provided to the universities: but it is not always wise to try to express notional economic measurements in terms of Exchequer money. The universities enjoy the occupation of buildings provided at public cost, and for this it would be possible to compute a notional rent. Students might be earning wages in production instead of studying, and for this it is possible to calculate an 'opportunity cost'. But nobody in their senses would add such items to university or student grants in order that they should be recovered by the Exchequer. The point is no more than a reminder that many activities have economic costs for which money does not change hands.

remembered, was gaining access to the details of university finance; and they began to ask pointedly whether the universities were being too passive about their mounting bills for rates. Were they not paying just what the rating officer asked, in confidence they would get it back from the UGC? Other rate-payers were not so lucky and had an incentive to fight valuations and demands that seemed unreasonable. The universities might need help with their rates – that was not in dispute – but if they expected that help from the Exchequer it was surely their duty to make sure that it was as little as possible.

Nobody could tell the Committee of Public Accounts that the figure for university rates, looked at in the whole context of Exchequer finance, was mere book-keeping designed to give the impression that universities paid rates; nor would it have been prudent to dwell on practical issues, such as the difficulty of arriving at the net annual values, if let to a willing tenant, of the Jodrell Bank telescope or the Bodleian Library.

So the universities went to work with a will disputing valuations. Experts were called in on both sides, and substantial sums were spent on their fees which would otherwise have been available for education and research. Test cases were mounted. Halls of residence were fairly easily rated as hotels if one disregarded the fact that they were not meant to earn a profit. Laboratories and libraries were more difficult. Nice distinctions had to be made about where medical schools ended and hospitals (not rateable) began. Animal houses, wind tunnels, examination halls, verged on the impossible. Were the sheds used in connection with teaching agriculture to be treated as agricultural buildings, and so disrated? But it was all done, and between 1964 and 1974 university rates went up from about £2m to over £13m a year. And it all continued to come from the Exchequer, and to be recovered, as far as possible, by adjusting the rate support grant.

These examples show how money spent on administration is often wasted, not through overmanning or incompetence but on tasks faithfully performed which would not be embarked upon, but cannot be challenged by, ordinary common sense. University fees provide another, and still more dangerous, illustration.

Once upon a time, as we have seen, tuition fees had provided an important part of university revenue, but as time went on it shrank to a negligible size. By 1959 fees were so trivial that the Anderson Committee had found no difficulty in recommending that in the case of mandatory awards (i.e. for all full-time British students reading for degrees) fees should be paid automatically from public funds direct to the university and without regard to parental means and this was duly built into the system of student support. Just the same, the fact that the UGC recurrent grant was a 'deficiency' grant designed to make up the independent income of autonomous institutions to a suitable level, still required that fee income – small though it might be – should be estimated at the beginning of each quinquennium and allowed for. It made no difference that most of the fee income came from the Exchequer by another route.

From time to time – usually when a quinquennium was nearing its end – the universities (through the CVCP) and the UGC would confer on the level of fees and arrive at a modest increase related to changes in money values. Neither side liked these discussions, mainly because they seemed so pointless. The fees had long since ceased to have any relationship with the cost of providing a course. They were much the same in cheap universities as in expensive ones. They were a book-keeping nuisance. Their value, at best, was as a symbol of the university's authority to charge fees if it wished. It never occurred to anyone that by the simple device of *assuming* a certain level of fees and expressing the willingness to pay them for British students through the awards system a Government could make the UGC recurrent grant exactly what it pleased and yet be able to maintain that the total income available to universities was perfectly adequate.

The Robbins Committee (or perhaps I should say Lord Robbins himself, since he exerted great influence on this point) saw fee income in a rather different light. It was always a tendency in Lord Robbins to value symbols of autonomy, and fees seemed to him to be such a symbol. The Report therefore urged a substantial increase in the level of fees to provide universities with 'an alternative source of income' to UGC grant. This suggests that the Committee may not fully have kept in view the fact that such a source was not in a full sense 'alternative' since the Government would always seek to ensure that the total of grant plus fees would be the same whatever the respective proportions provided by the two ingredients.

But the Robbins Committee urged another and quite different reason for increasing fees. It would impose a larger contribution on foreign students and their sponsors, and thus bring under control the large subsidy such students received from the British Exchequer.

It is not absolutely clear from the text of the Report that the Committee thought their two objectives would be best attained by increasing fees all round and then reimbursing the fees for the British (but not the foreign) students through the awards system; but that seems the best interpretation. If so, they proposed that a large fragment of the cost of universities should be met through a system of capitation. They might have suspected there was nonsense somewhere at the bottom of this when they were assured (as they record) by the chief Treasury witness (Sir Thomas Padmore) that an adjustment of this kind would present no technical difficulty. That assurance, as events have shown, was absolutely correct, but the readiness with which it was given might have been seen as a warning sign.

There was also an inconsistency between the two reasons given for the recommendation to increase fee income. The idea of an 'alternative source' really depended on a book-keeping transaction which would result in a nil alteration of public expenditure and the student 'not being out of pocket'. 'Bringing the subsidy to overseas students under control', however, meant that some overseas students and their sponsors would be (and should be) out of pocket. It might also have been noted that there were several other categories of students for whom awards were not mandatory (e.g. part-time students at such institutions as Birkbeck, and later the Open University) who would not benefit from the book-keeping transaction proposed.

This recommendation required a governmental response, and it is in this light that the Crosland decision should be read. It was part of the aftermath of Robbins, not a development of new thinking. Mr Crosland accepted the argument that the overseas subsidy should be brought under control, but rejected the idea of financing any part of the cost of universities by capitation.

The decision was made in the presence of two immediate pressures. One was that the UGC's proposals for financing the 1967–72 quinquennium were already before the Department and had to be settled as quickly as possible. Indeed the level of grant for the first year of the new quinquennium had already been announced (see Chapter VIII) and allocated to each university. Its huge total took account of no more than a vestigial fee income of the kind that had become traditional. A change in fee levels as a whole would therefore have meant recalling a large sum of UGC grant which had just been distributed. The second pressure was a peremptory demand from the Chancellor of the Exchequer, which had reached all Ministers during the autumn, for immediate and substantial savings, and this was currently being examined in relation to all DES programmes, with various unpleasant choices being generated as a result.

I have said 'all DES programmes', but it must always be remembered that most of what was spent on education did not pass through the hands of the DES at all: it was found from rates and rate support grant. In urgent economy exercises, therefore, attention tended to fasten on the services for which the DES was directly responsible such as school meals and milk, museums and galleries, research councils, student support and universities. It was far easier for the Secretary of State to operate directly on these than to spread any necessary saving more widely by imposing pressure for a relatively small economy on the managements of locally based education.

The concept of a large general increase in fees, despite the authority given to it by the Robbins Report, made no appeal to any of the interests concerned, and for a number of powerful reasons. The universities preferred the traditional low fees. The local authorities, who would have had to pay the higher fees in the first place, were suspicious that they would be short-changed when it came to reimbursement from the centre. Additional, troublesome administration would be needed. The UGC, however, had more profound reasons for disliking any substantial element by way of capitation in the financial support of universities, especially at a time of rapid expansion.

The UGC, after all, was presiding over, and responsible for, a gigantic programme which was in mid-stream. Control of it meant, among other things, setting a number of students at which each university should aim in successive years, and at the same time discriminating between institutions on grounds of expected capacity and variegated academic distinction. Some universities, especially the newer ones, cost more per head than others, for perfectly acceptable reasons. If one-fifth or more of the university grant was taken out of the hands of the UGC and paid by way of capitation the capacity of the UGC to control the programme would be seriously diminished. The incentive to pack in students (in the confidence that UGC grant, once fixed, would go on for five years) and so improve income beyond what the plan contemplated, would be irresistible to some universities, and their gain would be at the expense of those institutions which resisted the temptation in the interests of research and the maintenance of a high standard of entry, or simply because they had no room. To put this in more theoretical language, the UGC in opposing a general rise in fees was defending the very ground which the Robbins Committee had considered the most valuable of all:

the device of interposing between Government and institutions a committee of persons selected for their knowledge and standing and not for their political affiliation. In this way it is possible to ensure that the measures of coordination and allocation that are necessary are isolated from political influence. This device is exemplified in the present arrangements for the famous University Grants Committee.[3]

No persons selected for their knowledge and standing would be interposed between the universities and the authorities paying capitation at the rates the Government itself had prescribed.[4]

On the other hand the case for doing something about the fees of overseas students was very strong indeed. In 1964–5 they formed 10.4 per cent of the total number of university students, which was already more than the 10 per cent allowed for in the Robbins estimates.[5] In terms of absolute numbers they had increased during the previous ten years from 8,000 to over 14,000. The Robbins figure for 1973 to which the Government was committed would carry them to 21,000. The shortage of adequate British candidates to fill the large number of places being created in science and technology encouraged universities to fill them from abroad – especially at postgraduate level. It was estimated, in 1964, that British universities were supplying 10 per cent of the higher educational needs of Norway. At the London School of Economics 20 per cent of the students came from abroad, and three-quarters of them were from developed countries – mainly the United States and Canada.[6] The total cost of overseas students was about £9m.

There could be no objection to laying out such a sum in educational aid: but that is not what it was. Its incidence was from that point of view capricious. The subsidy went to many who could well afford to pay or had ample opportunities for higher education in their own countries. Its amount had no relation to overseas need or to foreign

[3] Robbins Report, paragraph 727.
[4] The UGC never expressed itself formally in these terms so far as I know: but that these were its thoughts I have no doubt whatever. The point about interposition is undoubtedly valid. Local education authorities had the power (admittedly it was never used) to withhold awards from students whose progress was unsatisfactory; and the Government could certainly have put a unilateral limit to the number of students for whom it would refund fees.
[5] In many of the technical colleges (which were on the brink of becoming polytechnics in a number of cases) the proportions were much higher. This was an important factor in the decision.
[6] Tessa Blackstone, Kathleen Gales, Roger Hadley and Wyn Lewis, *Student in Conflict: LSE in 1967*, Weidenfeld & Nicolson, 1970, p. 271.

policy, but was proportionate to an estimate of the demographic and economic needs of Britain. Moreover fees paid by overseas students constituted real money as distinct from Exchequer money conjured into existence for book-keeping purposes.

These were the grounds for the Crosland decision. It did not abolish the subsidy (and so, as it turned out, did not deter applications from overseas students) for the fee of £250 was less than half the average cost of a course.

I doubt if the universal outcry which followed the decision would have been less if the domestic fees had been raised at the same time and then reimbursed through the public purse. The hypocrisy of such a course would have been transparent, and the discrimination between home and overseas students scarcely less obvious. I do not think it was even considered. Nor do I think a blander and smoother presentation – not that this was considered either – would have avoided the storm. The reason for the all but universal indignation lay deeper, in the fact that the decision flouted important university and political realities.

The eyes of the DES at that time were firmly fixed on achieving a nationally accepted programme for the universities, but I do not think it fully understood how deeply international affiliations matter to the universities and those who work in them. Those affiliations spring from the fact that knowledge and inquiry in any subject are valid regardless of the geographical origin or location of the knower or inquirer, and this is expressed not only in the presence of students and staff from overseas in a nation's universities, but in innumerable institutional and personal links throughout the world. International reputation is a precious possession for a university and the highest aspiration of a scholar or scientist. Pursuit of it is therefore closely related to the very idea of academic autonomy and scholarly independence.[7]

A second reason for the affront caused to the universities was the unilateral character of the decision. True, the Government and the UGC had always had a voice in the level of fees, but constitutionally

---

[7] It is often argued that direct advantages accrue to Britain as a result of educating foreign students who later return to their own countries and positions of influence there as sympathisers with Britain, its people and its products. This is true, and can be supported by many specific examples. It is also the case that a British education does not always produce sympathy for things British and that loyalty to what is seen as the national interest will (and should) take priority over foreign educational background. I therefore prefer the more general formulation I have given. The deeply felt bond is scholarly, scientific and in a measure personal: not economic and political.

it was a matter for the universities alone, something which needed the approval of each individual university senate. Yet in this case their approval was taken for granted, and if withheld would carry a financial penalty. Several universities took their stand on this issue and for a time refused to charge the increased fees. Here university autonomy was in collision with the ultimate power of the Government, and the UGC had not prevented it. Indeed the UGC never gave any formal advice on the subject at all, either before or after the decision.

The affront to autonomy, which momentarily caused Vice-Chancellors and radical students to march shoulder to shoulder, was not the only fault in the decision. It failed to take account of the fact that the issue was at least as much one of overseas as of educational policy, including, in particular, decolonisation (then in full swing) and settlement in this country from abroad – a question which was among the most profound this country has faced since 1945. In 1966 thinking on this was still inchoate. The formers of policy on these questions lay outside the normal contacts of the Department of Education and Science in the Foreign Office and, particularly, in the recently created Ministry of Overseas Development, then headed by Barbara Castle and Sir Andrew Cohen.

This aspect of policy was not sufficiently explored at the time of the decision nor, I think, was it even understood. It can be clearly seen in retrospect that there are two main categories of overseas students: those who, on grounds of aid or of foreign policy, should receive a subsidy, and those who are seeking an education which they could get in their own countries and with or without sponsors could well afford to pay for. In either case the source of funds should be evident. In the first it should come from funds at the disposal of aid and foreign policy, and in the second from the individual. Finally there is the category – small, perhaps, but important – of foreigners a university especially wishes to admit, but who have neither the personal resources nor the claim of overseas aid to meet their expenses. This cost, and this alone, should fall on the institution concerned.

I had some discussion at the time with Andrew Cohen, whom I knew well, and I do not think either of us then saw what now seems to me so clear. That great man at first thought that an increase in the fees of students from abroad would produce no particular difficulty, that it was primarily a matter of educational rather than overseas concern, and as such was justified. Later, I think, he changed this opinion. But in the discussions surrounding the decision the only person to express alarm about what was proposed was the redoubtable Dame Nancy Parkinson of the British Council.

The long-running battle over fees has done great harm. It was not itself among the causes of the change from euphoria to despair which is the theme of this book, but it exposed an essential ambiguity in the relationship between Whitehall and the universities which the UGC system could not resolve. The existence of a fee structure became a constant temptation to Governments to carry out adjustments which by-passed the UGC. In the case of overseas students, whom the adjustments mainly affected, the universities were in effect asked to collect a tax which was not only cumbersome in itself and resented by those who had to pay it, but resented also by those who had to collect it since it was disguised as a charge which was made by their sole authority.

A solution would have to lie in a voluntary surrender by universities of their right to levy fees for any students, be they domestic or foreign, for whom provision is made from British public funds. The British students would pay no fees. Foreign students could then be liable to a tax levied by Government on all students seeking residence for purposes of study, and those who paid it, or had been excused it, would also not be liable for fees. There would be power vested in the overseas departments to excuse payment of this tax up to whatever limit was thought appropriate in the interests of aid to underdeveloped countries and overseas policy. There would be nothing to prevent British sponsors, including the universities themselves, from contributing to the tax for a foreign student who needed help and could not gain excusal. No doubt there would be some students who did not fall into any of these categories, and for these alone the universities, unimpeded, would set fees.

One such category would be the older, part-time student, probably in employment. Given that such students, important though they are, cannot expect mandatory grants and total relief from fees, they at least deserve sympathetic treatment for education in institutions which their society has provided. The cost of the course is no more relevant in their case than it is in that of the traditional full-time student straight from school, and is best related to the ability to pay. A proportion – say 10 per cent – of net average earnings would not seem unreasonable for the investment these students make.

At any rate a solution along these lines would save much administration in universities and place costs visibly where they belong.

Pursuit of the consequences of the Crosland decision of 1966 has led me out of the general sequence of events. It led to what was undoubtedly the first general upheaval of university protest this country had experienced for many years. Lord Longford, as the Government spokesman seeking to defend it in the House of Lords, found himself virtually in a minority of one among the speakers. Motives of racial prejudice were the subjects of denunciation on university campuses. In this respect it was a fitting preliminary to the turmoil that was very soon to break out in the universities. Yet in fact, as we shall see, it did little if anything to precipitate it. The elements of it had occurred at Berkeley, California, some time earlier, and so far as Britain was concerned they were being matured at LSE some six months before Crosland made his announcement. The real importance of the controversy lies in the glimpse it gave of the power of Government – also without being aware of it at first – to circumvent the safeguards of the UGC system which had been installed in conformity with the Robbins Report.

X
Student Power

Just two months after the signature of the Robbins Report President John F. Kennedy was struck down by an assassin. His policies in Vietnam and for the expansion of higher education were continued and extended by his successor, President Lyndon B. Johnson.

International emulation had been one of the most important arguments advanced by the Robbins Committee for the expansion they advocated, and of their numerous visits abroad to examine foreign systems their two longest had been to the USSR and the USA. They had been deeply impressed by the massive programmes they found in both those countries, and after making all allowances and qualifications on grounds of standards, failure of students to complete courses, and the unfamiliar gradations of institutions, there is a note of envy in their conclusion that 'when we look at what is planned for the future, the comparison between this country and other higher developed countries is ... disquieting'. Indeed the proportion of each age-group in the United States completing higher education had long exceeded what is was in Britain.

President Johnson's manifesto for 'A Great Society' appeared shortly afterwards. I read it in combination with Clerk Kerr's *Uses of the University,*[1] and with a sense of misgiving. It seemed to me that such gigantic educational schemes depended on assumptions about human behaviour on a scale which had not been considered, and that if those assumptions were falsified even to a small degree the resulting distortions could be on a very large scale indeed. It also struck me as incongruous that such a grandiose expansion of higher education should be undertaken at the same time as a dangerous, difficult and distant war whose context was utterly remote from academic values.

I begin this chapter with these references to the wider world because the student turbulence that now began to afflict the universities was not only in itself an international phenomenon but also drew many of its campaigning issues from world events such as the Vietnam War and the general rejection of the colonial system with its attendant racial

[1] Clerk Kerr, *Uses of the University*, Harvard University Press and Oxford University Press, 1963.

connotations. These indeed were issues which directly affected many students and would-be students, but I do not think that either the issues or their impact on students can be regarded as the source of the turbulence, though its seeds were carried from one country to another, and originated in the United States. The causes are to be found in the sheer scale of the expansion itself and the fact that it was undertaken in open societies. In the USSR the scale factor was present, but not the openness, so such beginnings of outbreak as occurred could be muffled and as a result stunted.

Although the Robbins Report devoted a chapter to 'Teachers and Students', and another to 'Internal Government', it had nothing to say in either about the problems of discipline, management and social stress which might result from the creation of a new class of social beneficiary on an immense scale in the heady atmosphere of higher education. The underlying assumption clearly was that the existing structure was capable of rapid expansion without any real change. Student unions, participation and all the scenery which was so quickly to obtrude on the public gaze receive barely a mention. The chapter on 'Teachers and Students' ends with a benevolent warning that to be either was a privilege, and leaves it at that.

But the new class of social beneficiary was not like the earlier classes created by the welfare state. Its members were neither old nor sick nor unemployed, but young, energetic, intelligent and full of expectations from life. They had been recently told that society had undertaken vast commitments on higher education because the future of society depended on it, so the very arguments that had brought them into existence as a class caused them to reject, or at any rate not to accept, the idea that they were beneficiaries. As David Adelstein, one of the ablest of the student leaders, put it:

The student who regards his study as a privilege or a means of social mobility is likely to be very passive towards the system, to assiduously learn what he is told, never questioning its validity. In contrast, the student who takes higher education as a right will respond much more assertively. He will demand his 'rights' adopting a generally critical approach to all he is taught or expected to know.[2]

Nothing infuriated students at that time more than to be told they ought to be grateful. The general public, on the other hand, was inclined

[2] David Adelstein, 'Roots of the British Crisis', in *Student Power*, edited by Alexander Cockburn and Robin Blackburn, Penguin Books, 1969, p. 78.

to think they should be. The rift thus opened up was to have lasting consequences.

The British university system had certain characteristics that moderated student turbulence, others that enhanced it. The staffing ratios were favourable; the standards of selection were high by international standards, so failure rates were low; the physical facilities were enough to prevent the accumulation of deprived hordes of students such as appeared in the 'democratised' universities of the Continent: all these had a moderating effect. The claims of overcrowding and discomfort, though made, were, I think, exaggerated.[3]

Against all this was the result of the doctrine strongly enjoined by the Robbins Report and tenaciously supported in the universities by staff and students alike, that students should by preference study at institutions well away from their homes. It took students in large numbers away from familiar social surroundings to become academic atoms. They were unbonded proletarians, free, young, uncommitted.

Then there was the reverence for the autonomy and independence of the universities, which had been the strongest theme in the Robbins Report. One of the most important incentives of student Jacobinism was thereby provided. Its purpose is often seen as the destruction of university authority, but that destruction – as the slogan 'Student Power' itself teaches – had the further purpose of capture, after transformation, of the power which had been publicly and solemnly conferred. According to some enthusiasts the remainder of established society would gradually give way once the bastions represented by the universities had been captured, and the whole would fall into the vision of anarchic concord symbolised by the sit-in. But for the great majority the university was the world, and it was a sufficient objective to wrest from the existing possessors of its government the treasure of university autonomy. The revolt was therefore intramural and was fought within the landscape of autonomy, much of which favoured the rebels.

University campuses and buildings had not previously been thought of as battle-grounds, but their very size and character made them ideal for the purpose, and perhaps a generation which had never experienced war except on television, and shrank from it, nevertheless needed to

---

[3] I have seen more university accommodation than most people, and have usually been shown the worst. Some of it was very bad indeed. But that is not the point I am making here, which is that poor accommodation was not a factor making directly for turbulence. The companionable conditions of a sit-in were far more austere than even the roughest student accommodation I have seen. It was a matter of what people felt about their surroundings.

express that side of the human character which finds an outlet in the comradeship, danger and excitement of war. Many of the student heroes were in fact military men – Castro, Che Guevara, Trotsky, Giap, the Mao of the Long March. But the picture of war they provided was different. The clumsy uniformed hireling enemies would tumble from the saddles under the well-directed fire of the ragged but devoted guerilla fighters. A campus – large, complicated, continuous, isolated – made a perfect campaigning ground for the imaginative strategist. It lacked any permanent garrison by the opposition, and it could be cut off, picketed and exhibited. It was in fact an ideal theatre of war.[4]

The only official connection between Whitehall and the student world lay in the subject of grants, and this was the concern of the established student organisations. These were traditionally regarded in Whitehall as much less significant members of the circle of consultation on the grants system than the local authorities who administered the grants. Soon after taking responsibility for the grants system at the DES in 1964 I received a letter with a cyclostyled signature from the National Union of Students inviting me to attend their annual council as an observer, and was assured by the old Ministry of Education hands to whom I referred it (they still manned that division) that it was a mere matter of form and was never accepted. I nevertheless felt some gesture was needed and invited the NUS officers for an informal talk with me and the head of the awards division, who was also a new broom from another department. At the end I made the mistake of offering them a glass of sherry, whence derives, I fear, the pejorative phrase 'sherry-party diplomacy'.[5]

Then, and for some time afterwards, the NUS management was very much in the hands of a caucus based on Queen's University, Belfast. Its members were mostly in their middle twenties and well understood, from their Irish experience, the dangers posed to university life by politicisation. They therefore defended the rule in the NUS constitution which excluded political pronouncements, and fell from

---

[4] If this is doubted, one should consider the difference in the publicity achieved by a sit-in as against a street demonstration. From the time of the Berkeley disturbance onwards the student strategists made emotional objectives out of physical features within the university precincts. An example is the refusal of the LSE authorities to allow a student meeting in the Old Theatre to protest against the appointment of Adams as Director, which was immediately stigmatised as a ban on free speech. It was not. The meeting could have been held anywhere but in the Old Theatre. There is nothing like reducing the enemy to defend a position of no strategic value to him.

[5] Sometimes given the edge of corroborative detail as 'Tio Pepe diplomacy' in Jacobin student oratory. But I think it was amontillado.

power when it was repealed in 1968;[6] but they were still occupying the platform on the two occasions, in 1965 and 1967, when I did accept invitations to attend the annual council as an observer.

They were both held in mid-winter in the Winter Gardens at Margate. Grey mist and angry waves could just be perceived through the extensive glazing which gave onto the windswept esplanade, and made a strange contrast with the flowers heaped against the rostrum and the intense activity of the hundreds of delegates. They sat at innumerable coffee-tables, one of which was assigned to each institution represented. The federal character of the union was thus at once apparent. Manchester had a table, and so did Lampeter, though the numbers round it were different. A curious result of this was that the NUS, like the rest of the university world, paid tribute to the metropolitan universities of Oxford, Cambridge and London by giving each of their colleges separate representation: for these universities did not have monolithic unions like the others. London had unions for each college. Oxford and Cambridge had junior common rooms, each of which might (or might not) be affiliated to the NUS. Those that were, commonly had left-wing leadership, so that the coffee-tables occupied by Christ Church, King's and Trinity seated some of the most desperate Jacobins in the assembly. In the front row at the centre, conveniently near the platform, was the table occupied by the delegates of the LSE, among whom David Adelstein was prominent.

The formal proceedings continued haltingly against a fusillade of procedural objections and points of order, mostly aimed against the President's conduct of the debate or the committee that had drawn up the agenda. Far more stimulating were the informal proceedings which lasted from the evening adjournment to the resumption of business the following morning. All night long, for hours and hours, over beer, coffee and tea, the delegates milled about in discussion and intrigue with a sense of elation I shall always remember.

The NUS received more attention from the education Ministers of Crosland's time than from any of their predecessors, and Crosland himself managed to raise a cheer from the delegates with a derogatory reference to the Governor of California, Ronald Reagan, who was then involved in the first outbreaks of the student protest. But I do not think the NUS, even when it fell under the sway of the left, ever constituted the leadership or even the mouthpiece of the revolt when

---

[6] The 'student interest only' rule came under regular attack from the early sixties onwards. Its disappearance was a very important step in the politicisation of the NUS.

it came to Britain. It was too big and bureaucratic for Jacobinism to manoeuvre effectively, and it lacked articulation. The real battles were fought within the institutions on the stages provided by university autonomy.

Within a very few months of Crosland's scornful reference to Reagan the campaign at LSE was being planned.[7] It is not the purpose of this book to describe in any detail what happened at LSE and other institutions from 1967 onwards.[8] But certain features of it are so important for an understanding of the contribution that student tumult made to the change in the position of the universities that they should be referred to.

A highly charged political issue which was quite external to the institution – what was going on in Rhodesia – was woven, often with the flimsiest and most distorted materials, into a controversy about the School and its government. Mere demands for greater participation in that government would have made an uninspiring banner under which to advance towards the transformation and power of which the Jacobins dreamed. That path led to committees, procedures of consultation, minutes – a game which could captivate very few students and was played better by the other side. But let authority be confronted by a request in a context which appealed strongly to the student body, *but which authority was bound to refuse*, then there would be a response to the fiery cross. Then the dignified and liberal language of the Robbins Report could be used against the very authority it was supposed to validate.[9]

---

[7] See Colin Crouch, *The Student Revolt*, Bodley Head, 1970, p. 35. 'Towards the end of the academic year 1965–66 [i.e. in the summer of 1966] we therefore resolved that a demand for greater student participation in the running of LSE should be launched as a major campaign the following October.' He goes on to describe how two groups were set to work: one to make proposals for participation to the authorities, and the other to devise tactics for enforcing these proposals if they met with resistance. During the summer vacation a group from the recently formed Socialist Society, under the leadership of Adelstein, had independently begun to prepare material for the attack on Walter Adams, whose appointment as Director in succession to Sir Sydney Caine had been announced in June 1966. In October 1966 Adelstein's group published its attack on Adams and his appointment; and Adelstein was elected President of the Student Union.

[8] There is a copious literature on the subject. The primary material on LSE is to be found in two contrasting accounts: H. Kidd (then Secretary of the School), *The Trouble at L.S.E.* Oxford University Press, 1969; and *L.S.E. What it is: and how we fought it* by 'Open Committee, LSE Socialist Society', an *Agitator* publication, 1967. See also Tessa Blackstone and others, *Students in Conflict: LSE in 1967*; and Crouch, *The Student Revolt*.

[9] Adelstein was a most acute student of university politics as is shown by his essay 'Roots of the British Crisis', and he agreed with Lord Robbins, for instance, in condemning the binary system: 'A structural device cannot, by virtue of being officially decreed, change the present relations' (p. 70).

The form of government transmitted to the universities more or less unaltered through the Robbins Report had never been designed to cope with a skilful and determined revolt by the student body. Authority was on principle distributed behind a Maginot Line facing the only quarter from which it seemed possible an enemy might appear: the Government. Elsewhere the arrangements were those of peace and prosperity. The armour was rusty, the weapons of discipline blunt, the gunpowder damp, the troops (being for the most part recently recruited) unsure both of themselves and their cause. The authority of Principals, Vice-Chancellors and other senior officers had been carefully circumscribed, and ultimate power was constitutionally assigned in many cases (certainly this was so at the LSE) to unwieldy bodies whose elderly members often hardly knew one another by sight, and rarely met. The abler student leaders almost instinctively divined these weaknesses, which enabled them to fasten on any pockets of real resistance – often individuals – and overwhelm them in detail by vituperation, ridicule, calumny and obstruction.[10]

For a time the well-publicised spectacle of the LSE and other institutions in which existing authority was attacked in this way resembled nothing, perhaps, so much as the galleons of the Armada wallowing under the well-directed fire of Drake's smaller, darting ships. The honour and courage of the dons may not have been in question, but they were suddenly at a disadvantage.

The Government and Whitehall gazed on this scene as helplessly as if they had been the Duke of Alva and his army in the Netherlands. It is true that as student propaganda often pointed out there were many interlockings between the official and academic worlds. Lord Bridges himself was chairman of the Court of LSE when the trouble there started and he was succeeded by Lord Robbins: a tragic episode in that great man's career, for no quarter was given by his opponents, who by then were in full cry.

[10] 'What all this adds up to', writes Carl Davidson in 'Campaigning on the Campus', one of the essays in *Student Power*, 'is strengthening our ability to wage an effective "desanctification" programme against the authoritarian institutions controlling us. The purpose of desanctification is to strip institutions of their legitimising authority, to have them reveal themselves to the people for what they are – raw coercive power' (p. 349). Davidson was one of the most experienced student Jacobins and had been much concerned in the Berkeley revolt. His acute and frank essay echoes Clausewitz: 'Perhaps the single most important factor for the student power movement to bear in mind is the fact that the university is intimately bound up with society in general. . . . Every attempt should be made to connect campus issues with non-campus questions' (p. 345). His precepts (he duly became a full-time organiser for Students for a Democratic Society) have influenced many campus campaigns.

The separation of the universities and the state could not have been more conclusively demonstrated. Some parliamentarians demanded the place should be closed – later Essex became the favourite target for this. Letters were written to newspapers. *The Financial Times* asked rhetorically whether a governing body which included the Archbishop of Canterbury and the Editor of *The Economist* 'had failed'. A House of Commons committee perambulated the universities to find the cause of the trouble and came up with a singularly unilluminating report. But just as the police insisted the universities were private property into which they would not venture uninvited unless actual crimes were threatened, so the Department of Education and Science, in accordance with well-established principles, declined contact with – indeed recoiled from – the horrid scene.[11]

The UGC found itself in a particularly difficult position. As the nearest thing to an identifiable public authority for the universities (a role it always strenuously denied) it was naturally a target for both the student rebels and the increasingly vocal group that called for strong measures against them. But in the last resort its powers came down to those of the purse, and these could hardly be exerted against a management facing a student upheaval.

Sir John Wolfenden, however, did register one personal achievement which did much in the longer term to moderate the troubles and has endured. The traditional position in which the student body had no say whatever – not even a formal say – in university management was no longer sustainable, but there were manifestly some things which had to be under the control of the permanent, as distinct from the transient, members of the university community. He accordingly embarked on triangular negotiations with the National Union of Students and the Committee of Vice-Chancellors, from which emerged the so-called 'Concordat' which still governs the formal participation

---

[11] Attempts were made to produce the opposite impression – for instance a letter forged onto DES notepaper was circulated during the student troubles at Leeds implying that the Vice-Chancellor was in collusion with the Department. Some students even hoped the Department would supersede the university authorities (see Crouch, *The Student Revolt*, p. 54). But on the whole very little of the student fury was directed against either the Government or the Department. There were indeed demonstrations about grants, but they did not arouse the same passion as the domestic revolts. Even the decision on the fees of overseas students, though it appeared at a crucial moment in the LSE revolt, did not divert the students there from their set objectives of protesting against the appointment of Adams and the 'victimisation' of Adelstein and Bloom. I rather think this was because espousing that issue would have meant making common cause with the university management, which was strongly opposed to the Government's fees policy.

of students in the government of most British universities. It conceded seats on university councils and senates to student representatives; with the reservation that on certain matters the student representatives should be excluded. The most important of these 'reserved categories' was any consideration of matters concerning the staff.

Although that agreement has now been built into the constitutions of most university institutions in this country, severe outbreaks of the kind first demonstrated at the LSE continued to occur up and down the country, and the tradition thus established over several generations of students remains even today as a force in university affairs. The consequences have been lasting, even though the bid for 'student power' in its original messianic form failed as it was bound to fail.

Apart from its international dimension, which was very important indeed, as I have tried to indicate, there were I think four main causes for the turbulence breaking out when it did, and with such ferocity.

The first was the size and rapidity of growth during the first half of the decade, not only in undergraduates, who provided the crowds, but proportionately in postgraduates and recently recruited staff who provided much of the leadership for revolt and introduced the vacillation displayed in many cases by academic bodies. A flood had to be handled by managements who lacked experience of the problems they now faced (where, indeed, could they have gained it?) and indeed had never expected to have to face them, so rosy had been the picture of culture and learning which would result from the expansion. That growth in numbers threw up enough energumens and Jacobins to seize the opportunities of the times and energise a large part of the student mass. It was not just that the crowd drew confidence from their numbers: the student demagogues themselves found safety in their own numbers. In the past authority had been able to strike down isolated rebels, as Shelley had been struck down at Oxford, but twenty or thirty leaders in a single institution were not so easily got rid of, especially when they had ample publicity and, through the union, could control funds and premises within the institution itself.

Their position was further strengthened by the development of a system (known as 'sabbatical years') under which the Presidents and other officers of the student unions were excused normal studies during their period of office (though their grants were continued) and were allowed a corresponding prolongation of their stay at university. Larger universities eventually had as many as five 'sabbatical' officers, and very few had less than two. Could it really be maintained that a student specifically exempted from the duty to study was subject to the normal academic discipline?

A second reason, which must be more tentative but is nevertheless plausible, might be found in the fact that by 1966 the expansion had brought into the universities a very large number of students whose home life had given them no impression of a university; and whose ideas were therefore derived from their teachers and from general reading.[12] The same was true, in a slightly different way, of a substantial body of staff who had no preconceived ideas about the university world, and were separated from the academic leadership by the gulf of the war years during which they had themselves been children. On this reading the struggle in the universities was not simply between generations, which is a constant factor in society. The cry of 'Pedagogic Gerontocracy' was thus ludicrous and was easily forgotten when the student generation chose to fasten on an elderly star such as Marcuse. Few students (and perhaps still fewer of the junior staff) believed the more extreme enthusiasts who preached that regular teachers could be dispensed with altogether. But the existence of a perceptible group of junior staff who were not (and perhaps on principle deliberately not) identified with their institutions to the same extent as their seniors was an important ingredient in the turbulence at LSE and many other universities.

Then there was the sense of what I have already described as 'elation'. The LSE student pamphlet I have mentioned calls it rather prosaically the 'sense of something happening that was far more important than lectures or examinations'. Colin Crouch is a bit more graphic:

It [the sit-in at LSE] was a form of mass participation activity which had broken down the existing structure of behaviour and created its own experience.

And again,

For a week we lived in a world of the eternal present, the heritage of the immediate past being destroyed and the future left to develop according to the dictates [an odd word when one reflects upon it] of constant spontaneity.[13]

---

[12] Table 2.4 of Blackstone and others, *Students in Conflict*, which is a breakdown of the LSE student body in 1967 by father's social class, does indeed indicate, as the authors say, that the great majority of the students were from middle-class families. But it also shows that 68 per cent of the students came from families not described as 'professional' – i.e. managerial, 'own business', clerical and manual. Bearing in mind the availability of university education a quarter of a century earlier it is a not unreasonable inference that very few of the fathers concerned with this 68 per cent had been to university.

[13] Crouch, *The Student Revolt*, pp. 55 and 56.

Student Power

Lastly, the Robbins Report and the surrounding debate had established that the universities (in a sense that was not applicable to the rest of the educational system) were at the same time enclaves in, but more than anything else part of, the social world. They were protected (not to say privileged) because of their peculiar importance, yet no institutions belonged more integrally to the generality. This paradox was quickly seized upon by the student Jacobins. Thus, ran the thought, which was easily communicated to the generality of students, the destruction of authority in the enclave would be an important step towards the transformation of society; yet those who inherited that authority would in a kind of way acquire the status the enclave provided. The doctrine of autonomy made a ring for the contestants in what developed as a civil war.

The student turbulence continued with greater or less energy for about seven years, and attracted as much attention as the Robbins Report itself. It did a great deal to negate the enthusiasm which had greeted that Report, and a stale, cold mood began to creep into public discussion of university questions. Those universities which suffered most severely, such as Stirling and Essex, found their application rates declining. The ruffled feelings of many ordinary people about the assault on what some students were fond of describing as 'the system' were eloquently expressed by the *Wood Green, Southgate and Palmer's Green Weekly Herald* commenting on one of the most celebrated sit-ins which occurred at the Hornsey College of Art:

The system is ours. We, the ordinary people, the nine-to-five, Monday to Friday, semi-detached, suburban wage-earners, we are the system. We are not slaves of it. We are it.[14]

Such disillusionment was not lost on politicians and civil servants. Treasury resistance on financial questions concerned with universities became firmer with the realisation that it was unlikely to be overruled on an appeal to Ministers. The inclusion of the university programme with those for hospitals and schools, which had become habitual in political speeches in the years immediately after the Robbins Report, ceased after 1967. The bounce went out of the programme.

But all this, important though it was, was a matter of atmosphere. There was virtually no administrative action by Whitehall in the wake of the LSE turmoil, no new decisions on policy. The 'Robbins Principle'

[14] Rescued for posterity, oddly enough, through a pamphlet published in defence of the Hornsey sit-in, whence it is quoted in Crouch *The Student Revolt*, p. 112.

remained emblazoned at the DES as a banner from which retreat was unthinkable. But the idea that it could be served more economically made rapid progress. The 'Fourteen Questions' asked by Shirley Williams soon after she became Minister of State at the Department of Education and Science in 1967 could hardly have been asked before that date. They included such challenges to the Robbins outlook as the possibility of two-year courses, longer terms and greater numbers of students working from home.

I have spoken from time to time about the 'high' and 'low' positions in university politics. In that parlance the students of 1967 were the academic Fifth Monarchy Men, Muggletonians and Anabaptists. They achieved the same magnetic conversions, inspired the same paralysis of will in their opponents – at any rate at first – and aroused the same revulsion in conventional society.

In the autumn of 1967 my own concern with universities was broken off by a posting to the Ministry of Health, and for five years I ceased to be involved in them. My post as head of the Universities Branch at DES was taken over by Ronald Guppy, on secondment from the Home Office. These changes were in conformity with the policy of giving senior officials wider experience, and I must confess that after seven years I was not altogether sorry.

XI

The End of the Beginning

Great changes occurred in the higher reaches of educational administration at the turn of the decade. In 1968 Sir John Wolfenden, who was approaching the end of his term as Chairman of the UGC, was offered a further term, but decided to answer a call to the directorship of the British Museum. He was succeeded, after an anxious search, by Sir Kenneth Berrill. Two years later Edward Copleston, who had sustained the UGC over more than a decade, retired from its secretaryship. In March 1970, Sir Herbert Andrew retired from the permanent secretaryship of the Department. Sir Toby Weaver, his senior deputy, followed him into retirement about a year later. In 1970, also, the defeat of Mr Wilson by Mr Heath at the general election brought an end to the term of office of Edward Short (who had succeeded Crosland as Secretary of State) and his replacement by Margaret Thatcher.

Sir Herbert Andrew was therefore succeeded by Sir William Pile shortly before the arrival of the new Conservative administration. Sir Herbert had I think been troubled by the idea of universities as the responsibility of Government. His non-interventionist approach suggested that institutions which were supposed to be autonomous and perpetual were unsuitable subjects for Whitehall. He shared the feeling of goodwill which many senior officials felt for the universities, and the idea of brigading them with the rest of the educational system seemed to him paradoxical. Sir William Pile was also sympathetic to the universities and understood the depth of their passion for autonomy; but unlike his predecessors for many years past[1] his career had been mainly in the Education Department, and he naturally saw the universities as part of the educational system he understood so well and had spent most of his life trying to improve.

Ralph Fletcher, who followed Copleston at the University Grants Committee, had worked all his official life in the Education Department, and had served as head of the part to which the Department rightly attached most importance: Schools Branch. Lean, gawky, bril-

[1] Sir Herbert Andrew had spent his career in the Board of Trade; his predecessor, Dame Mary Smieton, in the Ministry of Labour; and she had succeeded Sir John Maude, whose principal office, before moving to education, had been High Commissioner in South Africa.

liant, absent-minded, his life was tragically cut short in an accident in 1973, and I returned to university affairs as his successor.

By 1970 the greatest university leaders of the Robbins period were also being claimed by retirement or death. The two Morris brothers of Bristol and Leeds, Aitken of Birmingham, Mansfield-Cooper of Manchester, Knox of St Andrews, Logan of London, all ceased to hold their offices, or soon would do so. Both in the universities and in Government the approach to the new quinquennium due to start in 1972 was in the hands of a new leadership, under the shadow of the recent troubles and the pressures of alarming inflation. Between 1967 and 1970 the Brown Index of university costs increased considerably. It had not been fully compensated by augmentation of the grant, and expenditure per student in real terms fell from its peak by about 3 per cent.[2]

On 5 May 1970 the UGC addressed a letter to the universities to open discussion of the new quinquennium, and gave some indication of their own ideas for the future. It had the forbidding tone:

It is clear that at the end of the day the quinquennial programmes for which the Committee will be able to provide must aggregate to a total programme for the country as a whole, which is acceptable to the Government. . . . It seems probable that the settlement for 1972–1977 will contain strong pressure to reduce unit costs.

The aim was to be 320,000 students by the end of the quinquennium, with postgraduates contributing no more than the proportion they had already reached. The ratio of staff to students, which had already moved from a comfortable 1:7.6 to 1:8.1 might reasonably go to 1:8.5.

There was to be no further provision of buildings for science, and in the presence of the facts established by the Dainton Report the Committee thought that by 1977 a bare majority (55 per cent) for science students would be a rational aim. The money available for building had sadly shrunk. The projects to be started in 1971 and 1972 were to commit only £25m in each year – the lowest programmes in real value since 1960. There would therefore be discussions in detail about

[2] The figures are conveniently tabulated in Table 2 of Appendix VI to the *UGC Survey 1969–70*, which gives a ten-year run of average cost per student figures at constant prices:

	£
1959–60	752
1965–6	898
1966–7	900
1967–8	883
1968–9	864

the capacity of each university building, and:

it seems likely that the capital resources available for the the provision of additional residential accommodation during the next Quinquennium will be limited.

The gauntness of the UGC is understandable. As mediator it was no less its duty to tell the universities what it could see in Whitehall than it was to tell Whitehall what it could see in the universities. The letter was in essence preemptive, an indication to those on both sides of the divide that the Committee was not misleading the universities into expecting too much.

At the same time the Committee saw fit for the first time to issue a public document about itself. Such documents often mark a change of which the authors are not entirely conscious:

The universities are independent, self-governing institutions, usually established by Charter. They are free to conduct their own affairs, and they are not subject to legislative control or ministerial directive. On the other hand they depend on the State for the greater part of their funds; and they play an important part in the development of national policies and of the economy.

In this situation, if normal methods of control of government expenditure are not to be applied, there is a need for some intermediary between the State and the universities. There has to be some machinery which will enable public funds to flow into the universities without direct governmental intervention and which will reconcile the interests of the State as paymaster and the requirements of national policy with the proper academic freedom and autonomy of the universities.

This is very much how the Committee's position had been described in the Robbins Report, yet the language is somehow less sunny. There is a whiff – I am sure unintentional – of conditionality about the references to autonomy and freedom. But more important is the emphasis on the fact that the universities derive the greater part of their funds from the state as an obvious truth. Yet in fact the UGC had been in existence long before that situation arose.

The point at which UGC grant became the major source of income for the universities (probably soon after the War ended) had in fact marked a very important change which only became apparent gradually, because the UGC itself went on looking much the same. That change – as I have already mentioned – was ignored by the Robbins Committee, which seems to have looked on the exemption of the UGC and the universities from parliamentary audit as a specific privilege invented to safeguard university autonomy. It was nothing of the kind. It was the natural consequence of the ordinary rules of public accounting under which any institution receiving less than half its income from the Exchequer is outside the scope of parliamentary audit. Certainly the exemption was prolonged for many years after the rule would otherwise have applied, for reasons connected with safeguarding the universities, but that has already been discussed.

Looking at the university system as the 1967–72 quinquennium drew to a close, the UGC's main concern was erosion of its grant by inflation and the increasingly sporadic way in which this was compensated. In the later sixties the index of university costs (exclusive of the salaries of academic staff) was growing by more than 5 per cent, and in 1969–70 reached 11 per cent.

The 'index of university costs' does not measure the total costs of universities, which include the large sum devoted to academic salaries. When these were increased with the approval of the Government the appropriate sum was always placed at the disposal of the UGC; but the rest of what universities found themselves paying, which is the amount measured by the technical term 'university costs', had to be fought for. In fact it was more than half the grant and had grown much more quickly than academic salaries. A great deal of it (as I have pointed out earlier, in Chapter VIII) was salaries and wages for technicians, administrative staff, librarians, cleaners, porters, secretaries, counsellors, cooks, lodgings officers, sports advisers and caterers, whose salaries had advanced more rapidly than those of the dons. Other items were building maintenance, heating and lighting, books, chemicals, transport and office expenses, all of which were leaping ahead in costs, with the general realignment of rewards in society which characterised the sixties.

It was on this expenditure that inflation worked most damage. In the ten years between 1958 and 1968, during which the number of students had slightly more than doubled, the cost of academic salaries also slightly more than doubled, which illustrates the effectiveness of the controls, if not their justice; but the other costs rose by 150 per cent.[3]

The collapse of control over this area of expenditure, and (as we shall see) the reluctance and ultimate refusal of Government to meet the consequences, was the direct cause of the collapse of the traditional system for funding universities.

The Annual Surveys of the UGC during these years are filled with

[3] This can be readily calculated from Table I in the *UGC Annual Survey for 1968–69* (Cmnd 4261, HMSO, 1970), which shows the components of university expenditure over the previous ten years at constant (1967) prices.

concern over the growth of university costs; but one can scan them in vain for the slightest reference to the continued turbulence of the student body, which made a battlefield out of one university after another. The explosion at LSE had been followed, early in 1968, by outbreaks at Aston, Edinburgh, Leicester, Sussex, Essex, Manchester, Oxford, Cambridge and York. Then, in May, the all but revolutionary events in Paris put the student uprising on the world stage. 'When the Russians land at Dover', wrote Larkin about that time,

what defence for you and me?
Colonel Sloman's Essex Rifles and the Light Horse of LSE?[4]

In the succeeding years very few universities escaped serious trouble, and many of them had it more than once. Some savage outbreaks occurred in 1972, the most spectacular of that year being at Stirling, where the health of the Vice-Chancellor was broken and a fragile university brought to the brink of ruin; and at Oxford, where the university turned out to be a tougher proposition than its opponents had expected.[5]

Gradually the universities began to get the measure of their difficulties. The 'concordat' for systematic consultation with the student body and participation by students in decisions took away the most obvious grievance on which Jacobinism had fastened. Experience of previous battles taught Vice-Chancellors and Registrars how to deal with the next one. Several inquiries[6] into particular outbreaks pointed important lessons:

The possibility of maintaining order involves the possession of powers [said the Roger Young inquiry into the events in Stirling]; and universities increasingly find they do not possess the necessary powers when it comes to the point. . . . Few, if any, members of the university are prepared to accept the practical responsibility for maintaining order.

[4] The couplet is too apt not to quote, but I should record here how unfair I feel it to have been to the Vice-Chancellor of Essex University, who had to withstand a series of particularly ferocious assaults on his university. The details of the personal vilification to which he was subjected by students would hardly be believed. The wavering of many of the academic staff in support of this liberal Vice-Chancellor almost cost them the existence of their university through lack of applicants, and demands, resisted by the UGC, were made to close it.
[5] At Oxford the Jacobins (whose cause was the establishment of a Student Representative Council) seized a building in which to install it, calculating that the force available to evict them amounted to no more than half a dozen university beadles. Unknown to them the authorities had assembled from other university employees a 'territorial army' of beadles some sixty strong, ready to be called out in case of need. The fines and suspensions were also more severe than in most universities.
[6] Devlin (Cambridge 1972), Roger Young (Stirling 1972), Taylor (Lancaster 1972), Hart (Oxford 1974), Annan (Essex 1974).

Disciplinary procedures were burnished, administrative officers became more watchful, Vice-Chancellors conferred regularly with student presidents, press relations officers were added to university payrolls. To avoid the sudden jars, which every careful bee-keeper knows produce the angry swarm, authority began to move with gentle deliberation, as often as not accompanied by judicious puffs of smoke. A certain cost was involved – above all, of time – in reaching organis-ational decisions, and some such decisions, however desirable they might seem, were liable to be deferred. One of the most important consequences of the seven years' turbulence was a mood of caution, even anxiety, on the part of authority.

The trouble at the universities attracted most public attention during these years, but it was by no means confined to them. The art colleges were especially prone to turbulence. The new and rapidly growing polytechnics were also much affected, especially as they tended to lack the ballast of medical and scientific disciplines, and had come late, and somewhat under-provided, into the market for science students. Watchwords such as 'relevance' and 'accountability' did not save the polytechnics. True, the Jacobins among their students could not so easily raise their banners against ritual, tradition, gerontocracy and the holding of improper investments; but there were plenty of other causes to be found, notably in the curriculum itself. The buildings were often bleak or scattered; there was a notable lack of student resi-dence; and the provision for student unions fell far below what was found in most universities.[7]

The growth of the 'public sector' since the Woolwich speech had indeed been remarkable. By 1970–1 the number of full-time students following degree courses in further education was approaching 100,000, a figure far in excess of what the Robbins Report had allocated. Thus, while university numbers were approximately on the track proposed for them by the Robbins Report, the total numbers in higher education were greater than Robbins and his colleagues could have imagined in their most euphoric dreams.[8]

[7] Looking for historical parallels it is interesting to note that during a comparably turbulent era of British politics (1776–96) the institutions of higher education that were least affected by student disaffection were Oxford and Cambridge; whereas the liberal-minded and pro-gressive Dissenting Academies, many of whose staff sympathised with both the American and French Revolutions, suffered severely. The most famous of them – Warrington – actually had to close on this account.

[8] Table 44 of the Report (p. 160) proposed a total full-time student population for Great

The End of the Beginning

The polytechnics, which contributed most to this massive expansion of higher education outside the universities, were, as Crosland had said they would be, designedly different from universities in many ways. Control of their academic standards was largely entrusted to a central body (the Council for National Academic Awards) and only to a lesser degree to the institutions themselves; finance, and a great deal of administration, was the responsibility of the maintaining local authority and its officials; the academic staff were strongly organised in a different professional association from those in universities and had different rates of pay; and there was no direct central control over the total recurrent expenditure,[9] no block-grant system, no commitment for a period of years. The Committee of Vice-Chancellors and the Committee of Polytechnic Directors were separate organisations.

Since arrangements so very different from those used for universities were considered appropriate in what was now an almost equally large part of higher education, it became less easy to see that the arguments on which the Robbins Committee had commended the UGC system had as much validity as they had seemed once to possess. All that could be said was that they were well suited for institutions possessing autonomy. But autonomy was not just something the state had found in its path and felt bound to respect. It was claimed as a crucial safeguard for both academic respectability and responsible management, not as a mere historical accident affecting certain institutions which therefore had to be handled in a special way. If this were so, then surely it should apply to all institutions of higher education? If not, perhaps autonomy needed to be looked at more closely in the case of the universities. These unspoken thoughts lay at source of various kinds of ill-will between the two 'sectors'. The polytechnics resented the autonomy of the universities: the universities saw the regulated status of the polytechnics as a threat.

As time passed the polytechnics rebelled more and more against the restrictions to which they were subjected, and their demands for greater internal self-management became louder. The early attempts

Britain of 392,000, in 1973–4. Of these 219,000 were to be in universities. By 1970–1 the universities had reached 236,000, and the 'public sector' in England and Wales, including the Colleges of Education, 204,000. Of these 90,000 were in polytechnics and other further education institutions. See *Education: A Framework for Expansion*, Cmnd 5174, HMSO, 1972.
[9] This was due to the operation of the 'pooling' arrangements described on pp. 74 and 75 above.

that had been made to restrict their research activity gradually had to be abandoned. Whatever doctrines had given them birth they were being drawn insensibly in the same direction as the institutional waves that had preceded them – the civic universities and the colleges of advanced technology. Here and there the heads of polytechnics acquired such venerable titles as Rector and Provost, instead of the more workaday style of Director. Work for qualifications below degree-standard tended to shrink.

Outside the doctrinal sphere (which was concerned with maintaining the appropriate doctrine for each 'sector') there was virtually no coordination between the two systems. It was perfectly possible for the UGC to be discouraging the development of courses in universities in subjects for which the CNAA was validating new courses in polytechnics. Data were collected and presented separately, those for universities being much more informative. The two systems were the responsibility of two separate Undersecretary branches in the DES.[10]

Indeed one of the weaknesses the DES inherited from the old Ministry of Education was a tendency to organise itself on institutional rather than thematic lines. It is easier for officials to become experts in methods of finance and administration than in what is financed and administered, not just because they are administrators but because any informed display of interest on their part in the substance of what is being done is to invite accusations of interference. Attempts were made, from Sir William Pile's time onwards, to correct this tendency in the Department's structure, which is obviously inimical to coordination of policy. But progress on such a sensitive front is bound, shall I say, to arouse conflicting emotions in those administered, between desire for official effectiveness and suspicion of officialdom. Institutions are happiest dealing with 'their people' in Whitehall, rather than with officials who have to balance various interests, but this is on condition

[10] They came under the same Deputy Secretary, who was the only point in any hierarchy at which the two systems can be said to have converged. The Planning Branch, instituted at the DES by Sir William Pile, had to take two systems as it found them and allocate a share of student numbers to each. Scotland proudly said it had no binary system. There were Central Institutions directly financed by the Scottish Education Department, as well as Scottish universities financed by the British UGC; but the Central Institutions were more analogous to the small but important group of higher education institutions financed by grant from the DES – the Royal College of Art, Cranfield and the Open University. These never became the responsibility of the UGC but were administered by the same branch at DES as the one that corresponded with the UGC. Untroubled by binary doctrine they remained themselves and did very well as a result.

that 'their people' recognise the boundaries that must not be over-stepped.

The student intake of the polytechnics – as might have been expected by any reader of the Dainton Report – was not so much aligned to the sciences as to the arts and to social studies (including in that expression studies in management, business and commercial subjects). The science students were simply not available in adequate numbers, given the ample provision that already existed for science in the universities. From one point of view the gaunt and scattered polytechnic campuses performed the indispensable function of meeting the insatiable demand from well-qualified candidates for non-scientific courses; but that was not what had been expected from the original recipe.

In spite of these gathering clouds the traditional system for funding universities tacked steadily on towards the next quinquennium – the eleventh since the system was inaugurated in 1922. There was even an improvement, one might almost say a perfecting, of its procedure when, in 1970, agreement was reached between the DES and the UGC on a formula for regular supplementation of university costs against the inroads of inflation. The endless haggle would be ended. The value of the quinquennial grants would at last be guaranteed and the quinquennial system would again underpin confidence and autonomy as its designers had intended. Any perceptible movement of the Brown Index in one year would attract automatic supplementation in the next.[11]

Very soon after the arrival of Mrs Thatcher as Secretary of State the Department set to work on a comprehensive document about the future of education from nursery school to graduation, into which the UGC's quinquennial submission was fitted and in which it received its response. For the first time the attempt was made to include universities in a general educational plan, where resources were allocated to different services over a longish period to come. In this sense the White Paper *Education: A Framework for Expansion*[12] is one of

---

[11] The system has since become familiar as the basis for indexing social security benefits. If the Government is serious in its opposition to inflation and achieves a down-turn, the recipients of the formula gain: but if inflation continues indefinitely upwards the recipients are steadily impoverished. In the case of the universities the 1970 formula contained an additional safeguard for the Government, in that it guaranteed only 50 per cent of the loss of value absolutely, and offered no more than the sympathetic possibility of finding the other half. However, full compensation was given for 1970–1 (£8.35m) and 1971–2 (£13.1m), and was promised for 1972–3.

[12] It was published in December 1972.

the most ambitious documents of its period, and corresponded to what the educational world had long wanted to see.

The 'Robbins Principle' of access to higher education was not only firmly endorsed, but boosted, and the new aim was to achieve opportunity by the end of the decade for 20 per cent of eighteen-year-olds. Certain lessons of the sixties had been learned. For instance the justification of higher education was not 'manpower planning' – now detected by Whitehall as the will o' the wisp it was – but 'personal development'. This thought was alloyed with a warning that not all personal development was best achieved by study to degree standard, so intending students (and their advisers) were asked to consider motives for their aspirations. The need for students to leave their native surroundings and be provided with residence was questioned, and it might well have been added that one of its principal historical justifications had long disappeared, since hardly anyone now lived more than sixty miles from a university and the great majority were within daily travelling distance.[13] A damper was applied to postgraduate studies – something which had already been mentioned in the UGC's letter to universities. In fact some of the euphoric trappings of the Robbins Report were being dismantled in the interests of maintaining and improving progress.

Most notable of all the concessions to experience made by the White Paper was full acceptance of the lessons of the Dainton Report. Arts, even in the universities, would grow faster than science, and the plans allowed for a fall in the proportion of science students to 47 per cent by the end of the decade. But in spite of all these elements of caution and realism the White Paper fully lived up to its expansionist title. The aspirations of the Robbins Report in terms of numbers were made to appear modest by comparison. Those had been for a total, in all forms of higher education, by 1981, of 558,000. The White Paper substituted 750,000 – more than one-third higher.

This important feature of the paper rested, I think, on three judgments, the first of which was that numerical growth in higher education still commanded the degree of broad popular enthusiasm that it had elicited eight years earlier. We are not in the world of precise measurement on a question of this kind, but I doubt if this was correct. The

---

[13] The policy of providing residence had such strong social appeal that it was pursued without any regard whatever to the multiplication of institutions; and anyone who had suggested that one good reason for new institutions was to reduce the need for displacement of students would have been regarded as advancing a very strange argument indeed.

student troubles had had an unfavourable effect on public opinion, even though many excused or condoned them. The costs were beginning to be realised and even exaggerated. And on the credit side a fickle and impatient public did not see, or affected not to see, the general improvement in the economy and social life which had been held out as the reward for expanding higher education.

The second underlying judgment was that average UGC grant per student could continue to drift downwards. As we have already seen this had in practice been happening since 1968. The White Paper, which for the first time was used actually to announce the figures for the new quinquennium, set £252m for its first year and £309m for its last. On the number of students assigned to those two years the average unit of grant sank from £1,070 to just over £1,000.

This reliance on downward drift is colourable. After six years or so of improvisation and upheaval, experience might be expected to improve efficiency. The structure and the machine would shake down.[14] Less residence, a damper on postgraduates, a tilt towards arts, some tightening on staff, more effective use of space – all these would help towards the ministerial and departmental hope of more students for less money per head. But this would have implied a future of gentle growth and consolidation. What was offered was yet another decade of improvisation, innovation and the problems of rapid growth.

The third judgment was that higher education outside the universities, and especially the polytechnics, should advance with unprecedented celerity. The size of the task set to the polytechnics and other further education colleges is not immediately apparent from the text of the White Paper, and needs elucidation. In the year of the White Paper the total number of students in higher education in England and Wales outside the universities was 204,000, but of this total well over half (128,000) were in colleges of education. The colleges of education, however, were the one part of the system which the White Paper

---

[14] There are important exceptions to the idea that maturity and economy go together. One of these, when a service is expanding, is the cost of incremental scales, which means paying more each year for the same staff. The justification for this is that experienced staff are more valuable (though this value may take the form of a higher standard, rather than a diminution in the number of staff required). However that may be, the cost of 'Simpson's Creep', as it was known from the name of the distinguished civil servant who identified it, grew steadily in the universities because of the large number of comparatively young staff taken on in recent years. In a fully mature system the additional cost of those rising to the top of the scale is compensated by their retirement and replacement by those recruited at the bottom. By 1970 recruitment was already beginning to thin out considerably; and retirements were also few.

of 1972, for good reasons, proposed to compress – it was only too clear that falling school rolls were going dramatically to reduce the number of teachers needed. So the 128,000 places for teacher training were to be cut in the course of ten years to not more than 70,000, and only this figure was 'scored' towards the non-university 'sector' in respect of the colleges. All the rest of the mountainous figure of 335,000 allotted to the 'public sector' in England and Wales had to be found in polytechnics and further education colleges which, at the time the White Paper was issued, already contained about 90,000 full-time degree students. In other words those institutions were asked to increase their numbers by nearly three times – from 90,000 to 265,000 – in ten years. This was a great deal more proportionately than the Robbins Report had called for from the whole system over twenty years.

I have never been sure about the grounds for this judgment, which had a profound effect on what followed, and not least in the universities. The traditional sympathy of the DES for the 'public sector' and the powerful lobbies it contained no doubt played a part. And having created the polytechnics the DES naturally wished to see them strong and prosperous. The disagreeable necessity of running down the colleges of education required not only a compensatory gesture but an opportunity of redeploying the capital resources which till then had been committed to them.[15]

What is certain is that the cost of expanding the 'public sector' to this extent was quite unascertainable. The universities could be, and were, told what their grants would be and the number of students those grants were meant to provide for. They were even, on that basis, told in the White Paper of the Government's intention to 'arrest' unit costs and move to a stiffer staffing ratio. Such general admonitions were also addressed to the rest of higher education, but in the absence of any systematic way of assessing or regulating its costs centrally, such as the UGC provided for the universities, there was no way of enforcing them or measuring their effect. The universities were told what proportion of their students should be postgraduates. The poly-

[15] It is interesting to compare the recommendations of the Robbins Report for 1981 with those of the 1972 White Paper (in thousands of students):

	Universities	Colleges of education	F.E.	Total
Robbins	346	146*	66*	558
White Paper	375	75*	300*	750

*Including Scotland, for which 40,000 'public sector' places were allowed in the White Paper.

technics were not – probably because the number of postgraduate students in polytechnics was not known.

One of the most noticeable features of the White Paper's discussion of higher education was the readiness with which it used student numbers as a kind of currency. The change since 1963 and the Robbins statistical display was barely conscious – it was certainly unargued – but it was significant. The Robbins figuring had been in terms of 'places needed': that of the White Paper was in the form of human (if undesignated) units which were apportioned to the various 'sectors' with the implication that resources would be allocated accordingly. My emphasis on the distinction between numbers and physical places may seem at first sight pedantic, since a perfect fit is the natural (if unattainable) assumption; but on further consideration the distinction will be found interesting. 'Places' imply a verifiable level of provision, whereas 'numbers' do not. The seller of university education thinks in terms of student places; the buyer in terms of student numbers.

The danger of the currency of numbers is therefore its divorce from any measurable relationship to resources. It is possible, of course, to have endless discussion about the cost of creating or maintaining a university 'place'; but at least it will imply some additional resources. An allocation merely in terms of numbers could, at the extremity, have as its inducement no more than relief from an actual reduction in resources which would otherwise be imposed.

I do not think – and certainly I have no evidence for thinking – that this conceptual change was deeply designed. Nevertheless it shows that the initiative in costing had shifted, in accordance with the public mood, from the seller of university education to the buyer; and the inevitable tendency of a buyer, especially if he is the public buyer, will be to keep the unit cost of what he is buying (in this case the education of a student) as low as possible when he wishes to buy a large number of units. So the larger the number of units that was thought politically and socially desirable, the greater would be the pressure from the paymaster to reduce costs per unit. After all, he was still spending in total more than ever before.

The 'numbers game' was (and is) particularly dangerous when it was played in individual institutions. Within the university system taken as a whole the UGC could and did mitigate the effect of shrinking unit costs – if need be by insisting that the proposed numbers could not be reconciled with acceptable standards. But an institution that chose to make numbers its prime object in the interests of growth and apparently expanding income often committed itself to outrunning that income in the longer term; and this, even if accompanied by managerial stringency and deterioration of services, could not fail – bearing in mind that much the greater part of their expenditure was fixed – to bring them to the brink of insolvency.

All this is a proem to the next chapter and events which had their origins altogether outside educational policy. Considered on its own the White Paper of 1972 was the most vigorous assertion of the two major decisions of the past decade: the Robbins doctrine of access to higher education and the 'binarism' of the Woolwich speech. It was greater in its sweep than either of these utterances, but it still concentrated, as they had done, on the forms of the educational system, on the institutions and institutional interests that made it up. It had little to say about matching education to the generation for whom it was being provided. Nor were the needs of subjects, whether seen laterally through institutional 'sectors' or vertically through the different stages of education, considered as appropriate for pronouncements by the state.

Many of these anxieties occurred to the universities, or to people in them, at the time: just the same the system entered the new quinquennium of August 1972 in reasonably high spirits. How should the universities have known that high officials had regarded even the quinquennium of 1967 as something of a miracle? The new one had been achieved on an ascending curve attuned to still further expansion. The problem of inflation seemed to have been solved by a firm compact to index costs. Student turbulence might not have died out, but ways of containing were being found. The enlarged systems projected in 1963 seemed to be shaking down.

XII

The Beginning of the End

The huge system was by now very fragile, and in the first eighteen months of the new quinquennium it received two crippling blows.

Between the announcement of the grant and the beginning of the quinquennium of 1972 university costs and salaries rose by about 20 per cent and the indexing guarantee was called into play. The sums were agreed[1] and the distribution was made at once by the UGC on the enhanced basis.

During the winter of 1973–4 the nation was plunged into a crisis on a scale not equalled since 1956, perhaps since 1939; but unlike those crises it was not an external but an internal convulsion, erupting from many years of social and economic change. The universities had not been exempt from earlier tremors that preceded this earthquake, as we have seen from the adjustments made to the building programme at moments of pressure on public expenditure. But this time the blow cut deeper, since it was dealt to income. Early in December 1973 the Chancellor of the Exchequer, Mr Barber, announced large reductions in public expenditure, one of which was the cancellation of half the recently agreed compensation for increased university costs from 1974–5 until the end of the quinquennium. In doing this he expressed the Government's view (it was very much the Government's view since it had been arrived at quite independently) that 'these reductions could be accommodated without detriment to the planned growth of the universities'.[2] This would have been better left unsaid, if only because it implied that only a few months earlier the Government had been needlessly lavish.

This decision – apart from the supererogatory comment – was just within the contract. Full compensation for university costs other than agreed increases in academic salaries had never been guaranteed, since the Government had been careful to say that if it was strapped for

---

[1] The exact figures were: 1972–3 £50.9m on £252m; 1973–4 £48.5m on £265m; 1974–5 £51.75m on £265m; 1975–6 £54.75m on £292m; and 1976–7 £58.0m on £309m – a total of nearly £264m added to the settlement of £1,394m for the whole quinquennium made only eighteen months earlier.

[2] Cmnd 5519. White Paper on Public Expenditure, HMSO, 1973.

money the guarantee covered only 50 per cent of the reported increase. Nevertheless it was a reduction of about 5 per cent in what the universities had been planning for, and thought was already in their respective banks.

Worse followed in only a week or two – just before Christmas. 'Changes and uncertainties in energy supplies,' said the Treasury with a conviction that was only too understandable, required the cancellation of the surviving 50 per cent of compensation for university costs, and a reduction of nearly half in the furniture and equipment grants from 1974–5 onwards (these, as will be remembered, had been sensibly set up a few years earlier as separate from the main recurrent grant). So within the single month the universities suffered a reduction of 10 per cent of the resources they had been offered only a few months before.

I am willing to believe that up to that point the university system, like many other systems, was bloated; and its direct dependence on the Exchequer invited attack at a moment of national crisis. But the shock, not only of a 10 per cent cut but of the breach between the university and the state – the revelation that the traditional special relationship need not be respected – was shattering. No students marched, the whole thing was contained in flurried protests and agonised conferences in an atmosphere of power cuts and imminent collapse. But decisive damage had been done.

The fall of the Heath Government, which followed very soon afterwards, brought Reg Prentice to Elizabeth House, where the Department of Education and Science was now concentrated in greyish concrete and glass to a design which had been supplied, I believe, by Mr Poulson. Only just before this change of Government occurred it had been necessary to find a successor to Sir Kenneth Berrill, who had resigned the chairmanship of the University Grants Committee and gone on to become Chief Economic Adviser to the Treasury. The post was offered to Sir Frederick Dainton, who could be forgiven some hesitation in accepting it, for it was now one of peculiar difficulty and danger; and when he had been offered it on a previous vacancy, at a much more attractive time, he had declined it in the interests of the chair of chemistry at Oxford to which he had just been appointed. His acceptance this time was one of the few pieces of good fortune conferred on the universities for the hard world they were now entering.

The new Labour administration was neither politically nor personally unsympathetic to universities; and the Government had always represented itself as the friend of education in all its forms, especially, perhaps, of higher education. But two considerations acted on one another to make it resistant to restoration of the dramatic cuts made by their predecessors. The first was the enfeebled state of the economy, and the second a realisation that the esteem of the voter for the universities had declined. The counter-offensive launched by the UGC under its new Chairman therefore faced very great difficulties. This was the point at which, following the sudden death of Ralph Fletcher, I joined the UGC as its Secretary.

The counter-offensive was in some measure successful. First of all it was necessary to shorten the line by removing, as tactfully as possible, the now obviously overblown aspirations for expansion contained in the White Paper of 1972. Universities were at once told by the UGC that the number of 306,000 full-time students at which the quinquennium had been aimed was expected to fall short by between 8 and 11 per cent.[3] Never before in history had the UGC suggested such a thing. But this alone could not save the situation. All over the system desperate measures were being taken independently to match prospective commitments with resources. Almost every university imposed a ban on filling any vacancy which might luckily occur, however much a replacement was needed. Maintenance of buildings was postponed. Economy committees were set up to cut out frills and increase efficiency. Some remaining corpulence and easy money was squeezed out; but the atmosphere of panic and defensiveness that billowed forth was harmful and exaggerated. Essential posts were left unfilled in a mood of protest and defiance. Buildings were threatened with neglect. Small specialities were threatened with destruction by big battalions in academic committees, regardless of merit. These symptoms could not be cured by lowering aspirations in the longer term; they were damaging the existing quality of the system, and in many cases they went further than even the serious financial situation warranted.

Some immediate reversal of the dramatic cuts of December 1973 was therefore the other aspect of UGC policy, and after a fierce tussle between the UGC and Whitehall it was secured in July 1974. That campaign recovered about £4m a year for the universities, which was perhaps one-third of the amount that had been lopped off the compensation for inflation in university costs.

---

[3] This was an autonomous decision of the UGC. But in November of the same year the Government formally abandoned the ten-year aspiration of 750,000 students enshrined in the 1972 White Paper, and substituted 640,000 as 'still within the Robbins principle'.

A patch had been put on the side of the crippled ship. It was able, with a demoralised crew and very nervous passengers, to resume a limping course towards a rather more accessible haven than had been charted; but it was visibly lower in the water than it had been when it set out, and never again did the grant reach the level in real terms that had been proposed by the White Paper of 1972. Even that had envisaged a gradual decline in unit costs.[4]

The second serious blow to the university system in the year 1973–4 struck directly at the self-esteem and personal finances of university teachers, rather than at the financial system itself.

The new Labour Government had come to office with a pledge to carry out a fundamental review of the remuneration of teachers, and this was entrusted to a committee under the chairmanship of Douglas Houghton, since Lord Houghton of Sowerby. The purpose of this review was not merely to decide on improvements in the light of rapidly advancing inflation, or on some redistribution of rewards to the most deserving, to the most needed, or to those with particular skills and responsibilities. It was to remove a strongly felt sense of grievance that (in the words of the new Secretary of State, Mr Prentice) 'teachers have fallen badly behind in their pay and something must be done to help them'.

The lack of success with which the universities had really been engrafted – or accepted engraftment – into the official educational system was never more clearly exhibited than on this occasion. Here there was no question of a 'seamless robe' from nursery school to doctoral studies. The Houghton Report[5] has the curious title of *Inquiry Into the Pay of Non-University Teachers*, and as I remember the exclusion was not disputed by the university teachers themselves.

But the terms of reference *did* extend to teachers in the polytechnics, further education colleges and the colleges of education, right up to the highest grades. In considering this question the Houghton Inquiry emphasised the need to compare these teachers equitably with those in universities doing the same kind of work. But it was even more emphatic that its proposals taken as a whole had to respect the differentials throughout the system it was asked to consider. By and large

[4] The charts at the end of the *UGC Annual Survey for 1976–77* (Cmnd 7119, HMSO, 1978) show clearly what happened by comparing the path planned for the unit of resource compared to what it actually turned out to be. The reduction over the 'quinquennium' was just under 5 per cent.
[5] *Report of the Committee of Inquiry into the Pay of Non-University Teachers*, Cmnd 5848, HMSO, December 1974.

the increases were between 25 and 30 per cent, and these the Government hastened to carry into completion. The need to preserve differentials throughout the system conferred even larger increases on the most senior teachers in the 'public sector' of higher education. The maximum for a head of department was put up by 39 per cent, for a Vice-Principal by 46 per cent, for a Principal by nearly 50 per cent. All these increases were to run from the last settlement date of April 1973. As a whole these increases not only closed any gaps there were between teachers in universities and those in the rest of higher education, but carried the scales in the higher ranges of the 'public sector' far beyond those current in the universities.

The current scales of pay for university teachers were not quoted in the Report, though they were alluded to, and the impression was given that due regard was paid to them. But the fact was that the large increases for the general mass of the teaching force to which the Houghton exercise was committed did not correspond to any such comparison. From October 1974 the university teachers were due to receive an increase of about 8 per cent based on the previous year's inflation. They now demanded an addition of 18 per cent to bring them into line with the 'public sector'. Whether or not this was the right figure can be disputed, but there can be no question that it was not far out. The claim was refused on the ground that twelve months must elapse between settlements and a settlement for October 1974 already existed. Eventually the matter went to arbitration, which resulted in a finding favourable to the university teachers: but before that finding could be passed through the negotiating machinery the latest instalment of incomes policy ('The Attack on Inflation') subjected the university teachers (along with everyone else) to the views of Jack Jones of the Transport and General Workers Union, which offered a maximum increase of £312 a year to those receiving less than £8,500, and nothing for those above that figure.

Thus was born the celebrated 'Anomaly' which was not finally settled for many years and embittered relationships not only between the institutions and the Government, but between the individuals composing the institutions and the Government. The sense that the competitive 'public sector' which the Government had conjured into existence was being deliberately preferred made the disappointment much harder to bear. It was now clear that the universities were no longer the Government's favourite child.

This was reflected, as I remember, in the curious atmosphere of

unreality which surrounded the interminable negotiations over the
'Anomaly'. All three sides – the Government negotiators, the university
managements and the staff association – agreed it was there. But political considerations, in the broadest sense, prevented its solution. A
'special case' would now send tremors through the whole system. The
new universities, the transformed colleges of advanced technology, the
whole shining picture of 1964 had now, in the eyes of the Government,
shrunk in the public mind back to a Gothic image of 'Oxbridge' overlaid
by the University of Watermouth. This made things very difficult for
any sympathetic official who well knew the immense capital resources
that had been poured into the universities and the need (if only for
his own peace of mind) of preserving their autonomy.

Thus the threat to the traditional university system did not come
from ministries but from the gradual shift, or apparent shift, in the
public estimation of almost all national institutions. By 1973 the national
mood had progressed from the questioning, through the sceptical, to
the cynical; and in the case of the universities this was reinforced by
the realisation that although degrees were still valuable in getting
employment they were not, as in the days of a tiny university system,
the passports to secure and privileged positions.[6]

The universities were thus becoming fair game for political bargain-
ing in a way that would have been unthinkable ten years earlier, and
a further clear illustration of this is provided by the debate on regional
devolution which began under the Conservative Government of Mr
Heath and continued with passion into ultimate fiasco under the second
Government of Mr Wilson.

Mr Wilson himself had, in a statement made in Parliament in 1965,
set out arrangements under which the universities were to be treated
as a national system for the whole of Great Britain. The grants to
all of them, whether in England, Scotland or Wales, were to continue
to be made by the UGC, and ministerial responsibility for them was
to rest with the DES. The Secretaries of State for Scotland and for
Wales were to be consulted over the appointment of future members
of this national UGC, and the heads of all three Education Departments

---

[6] The civil service itself provides a good example. In the early sixties the graduate entry
had been mostly confined to the small numbers needed to maintain what was then called
the Administrative Class. By the early seventies large numbers of graduates were being
recruited into the lower grades which had formerly constituted the Executive Class. The
reforms of the early seventies certainly improved the prospects of those recruited at lower
levels; but they did not (and could not) make them equal to those formerly open to entrants
to the Administrative Class.

were confirmed as assessors entitled to attend and advise at its meetings. But the system remained essentially one for the whole nation, and very much the same as before.

The more enthusiastic devolutionists naturally saw responsibility for the universities in Scotland and Wales as an important function of the proposed new Scottish and Welsh assemblies. Some of them even slipped incautiously into the word 'control.' It was certainly said, along with this, that of course Grants Committees to assure traditional propriety would be installed at the same time in those countries. But to the national UGC and to many in the universities the claim rang hollow. What would be the point of devolving responsibility for the universities of Scotland and Wales if it were not to give those regional politicians and bureaucrats to whom it was devolved a greater degree of control than was exercised at present from the centre? Could it really be conceived that appointments, admissions, style, in the universities in Scotland and Wales would not become the close concern of regional governments and representatives? And if so, why not in England too?

There were other, more practical arguments against devolution, such as the national market for academic posts, the freedom of choice for students, the interpenetration and scatter of research interests and the position of the research councils: but the argument of autonomy, for which the UGC stood, was central, and university opinion both in Scotland and Wales was, on the whole, of the same mind in fearing what nearer nationalist administrations might do. The arguments within Whitehall were prolonged and difficult, since the point had been reached where in some minds the universities had become no more than small pieces on the larger political board; but the UGC view prevailed. Even before the collapse of the whole devolution scheme the universities were omitted from the responsibilities to be devolved.

The episode is instructive. The most important thing it showed was the way in which a political issue can affront university autonomy from an unexpected direction. The obvious directions from which the autonomy can be threatened are rarely the dangerous ones, or rather they only become dangerous if other political circumstances unconnected with the universities have cleared the access to them. Naked political influence over appointments, courses, admissions, if attempted by authority in its own name, can usually be headed off or exposed, and, although in my experience such attempts have occurred, they have been rare and uniformly unsuccessful. Private influence by persons in power, exerted directly on a university or on individuals in it, is another matter. Such persons inevitably have their own affiliations in the university world, and that world knows well enough how to deal with such approaches. It is not and cannot be isolated and insulated from the worlds of politics, business, the professions or the trade unions. How could it be and remain a university world? Autonomy includes the right to accept influence just as much as to resist outside authority.

On this issue, the UGC perceived its function to protect autonomy, and succeeded in carrying it out within the Whitehall machine. But this is subject to qualification. If the UGC had not had substantial support from Scottish and Welsh university opinion (and like any other university opinion this was not unanimous) it could not have succeeded; and if devolution itself had not collapsed in the ruins of parliamentary opposition and referenda I doubt if it would have been long before the new national assemblies would have demanded, and got, control of the universities in their respective countries. If that had happened the future in England also would have become an open question.

It had for some time been foreseen in Whitehall that the rapid physical expansion of the university system would draw to a close during the seventies, and the number of new buildings to be started would therefore decline. Much of the estate authorised in the years following the Robbins Report was only coming into use during the early seventies, and there would be scope, as time went on, for it to be used more effectively. So the official mind worked, and there was something in it.

But the tap was turned off with the utmost ruthlessness, and in ways which had notable effects on policy. One of the first acts of the incoming Government was to reduce university building starts of £30.6m authorised for 1974–5 to £11.5m, and this was to be the highest figure they were to reach for many years. For 1977–8 it was just over £6m and for 1978–9 it was £10.5m. These, as the UGC sadly commented, were the lowest figures in actual pounds for twenty years, and perhaps the lowest in real terms since before the war.

With its shrunken resources for capital the UGC was forced onto the defensive. It had to abandon any pretence of providing residence for students on the scale required by the traditional doctrine that the system should be treated as a single entity from the point of view of placement. The building of subsidised residence for students virtually ceased from 1973 onwards.[7]

[7] See Appendix V to *UGC Survey 1976–77*. No student residence scheme was fully grant-aided by the UGC after 1971–2. In that year a substantial number of places was provided by

The extreme shortage of capital enforced another important change in the picture of numerous self-sufficient, largely residential institutions with which the enterprise had set forth. The library is the heart and hub of a university, and considerable sums had been spent in providing them: but, even so, by the early seventies nearly half of the forty-four university libraries were either bursting at the seams or would soon do so if the existing policy of indefinite enlargement continued. At one great library (Manchester) books were being stored in basements subject to flooding. The UGC could not ignore such a situation, and it had no resources to cure it in the comfortably acceptable way. It commissioned a report[8] which came out with recommendations that would limit the rate of growth of on-campus holdings. The UGC commended the Report to the universities and then devoted almost the whole of its shrunken capital programme to extension of those libraries that were in the most desperate need.

The Report (usually known as the Atkinson Report, after its Chairman) hit the academic profession, which had already suffered so many blows, in a most sensitive spot, and aroused great indignation. Its logic was ineluctable, its remedies reasonable, but it marked the end of something precious. It was one of the milestones on the road to discovering that a large university system dependent on public funds would find itself sooner or later subject to controls which a smaller system had escaped. Nevertheless I think now that the UGC should have adopted the Atkinson Report for its own guidance, instead of commending it directly to the universities. The effect would have been very much the same to the extent that the UGC would have declared that it would help no library project from a university which did not accept the Committee's policy; but this would have left open to a university the possibility of seeking benefaction elsewhere and avoided at any rate the appearance of imposing a policy which was bound to set up resistance.

I now come to a series of transactions which transformed the basis of recurrent grant and considerably weakened the position of the UGC in relation to both the Secretary of State and the universities.

loans from the UGC (which of course had their effect on the rents charged), but even these declined steadily over the following years. Yet, surprising as it may seem, the total residential places provided (some 34,000) between 1971 and 1977 was almost the same as the total growth in the student population. Private benefaction began to play an increasingly important part.

[8] *Capital Provision for University Libraries. Report of a Working Group* (appointed by the UGC; chairman Professor Richard Atkinson), HMSO, 1976.

It will be remembered from Chapter IX that great bitterness had been aroused by Crosland's decision, in 1966, to levy a higher rate of fee for overseas students. Such had been the wounds given and received in that controversy that the fees then fixed remained current for nearly ten years, when Mr Prentice, formerly Crosland's deputy and now himself Secretary of State, was emboldened to add £70 to all fees, bringing the domestic rate (paid through the awards system) to £140 and the overseas rate (paid by the student himself) to £320. This occurred in March 1975, and slightly narrowed the apparent gap between the two rates. It also meant a downward adjustment in UGC grant, which was what the Treasury wished to see.

This move had been anticipated by the UGC and the Committee of Vice-Chancellors, who set up a joint working group under the chairmanship of the Vice-Chancellor of Leicester, Sir Fraser Noble, to consider the whole question of fees and see if it could be brought to some kind of reason. Such a joint working party was unprecedented, and marked the seriousness felt by both the UGC and the CVCP about the issue.

That study group took a long time to reach its conclusions, and while it was deliberating Reg Prentice departed, and Fred Mulley took his place. After a year's discussion the study group, in an interim report, proposed that the two rates (home and overseas) should remain, and be indexed by the index of university costs, which in that fatal year was 30 per cent. The Secretary of State (in July 1975) duly agreed.

But he was already experiencing strong pressure for even higher fees – at any rate in respect of overseas students and the many thousands in the 'public sector' whose fees were not paid from public funds. The number of students from abroad was steadily increasing, as one would expect, since the fees fell far short of the cost of their tuition.

In the early summer of 1976 the Noble group reached their final conclusions. The two rates should remain; they should be indexed; and there should be a modest increase in the overseas rate. Mr Mulley was in a dilemma. He could now for the first time claim respectable university support for a dual level of fees; but the overseas level proposed by the Noble group was far short of what was needed to meet the Chancellor's demands.

Mr Mulley's decision was that fees throughout higher education at degree level should be £500, and that all British students with mandatory awards should have this sum paid for them by public funds. The UGC grant was abated accordingly, and the claim was made that discrimination was now at an end. It did not last long, even for those who believed it. Mrs Williams succeeded Mr Mulley not long afterwards, and in 1976 raised the overseas rate to £650, leaving the domestic rate where it was at £500.

Three fee changes, three consequent adjustments in UGC grant to each university, all within two years, created arithmetical havoc throughout the system. The importance of getting the numbers admitted to each institution precisely right was enormously enhanced, for too few would mean significant loss to the institution and too many would bring down the wrath of the UGC. Committees to consider hardship to overseas students already on course were set up on every side. The money merry-go-round had taken off in deadly earnest. In its survey for 1975–6 the UGC included a paragraph about fees that was so tight-lipped that it did not even mention the levels proposed, and said simply that certain proposals had been made by the Secretary of State and modified in the light of UGC representations.

These successive decisions, which were all ministerial in character, paved the way towards what ultimately happened under the Government of 1979, namely full-cost fees for overseas students – a course which the preceding Government also studied. They also undermined the most important function of the UGC – its discretion to distribute funds to the universities; for the capitation represented by fees now became so large a part of university income that it was on the way to becoming as important as what issued from the UGC. Its power to differentiate between one university and another, or to control the number of students each should admit, was substantially impaired. The measure of capitation income could be fixed by the Secretary of State at any time, and could in theory dispense with the UGC altogether. 'Formula financing' was anathema to the UGC. Control over fee income by the Secretary of State introduced the simplest formula of all – a count of heads.

The trend towards capitation was the more alarming on demographic grounds. The immediate prospect for student demand in the seventies was upwards; but beyond that, when one came to the early nineties, it was clear that the age-groups from which students were drawn would decline rapidly. This did not necessarily imply a decline in student demand or a running down of the universities, but it brought out a divergence of interest between the Government and the UGC which has remained. In what I have called the Augustan period there had been a community of interest in the presence of an undoubted bank of human demand for university education. Government gained credit by providing for it, and the universities prospered.

But might it not be the case, it began to be said, that with a decline in numbers only a few years ahead, the increased numbers in immediate prospect could be squeezed in now at very little extra cost? Then, as the pressure relaxed, things would be more comfortable once more, research could again raise its head, overcrowding would be a thing of the past. This doctrine was known as 'tunnelling through the hump'. There was great argument about just how high up the mountain the tunnel should start; but the main reason for distrusting the whole approach was that wherever it started the traveller through the tunnel might not receive his reward at the other side. The unit of resource, once depressed, might not recover simply because there were fewer students.

This question was at the centre of the second official review of the future of higher education since the Robbins Report. 'Higher Education into the 1990's', as its title suggests, was the first governmental attempt to look beyond the horizon to which the Robbins arithmetic had been limited; and it had to do so without either the prospect of age-groups expanding in the immediate future or a mood of optimism. Begun under the auspices of Mr Mulley and completed under those of his successor Mrs Williams, it is a much less assertive document, both in appearance and style, than the products of either Lord Robbins or Mrs Thatcher. It contains no vibrant phraseology or policy decisions and its manner is tentative, even apologetic. It was modestly known as the 'Brown Paper' and was not even printed, though it was widely distributed. 'The five Models described in this paper', it says humbly, 'are not so much policy options as the strands out of which a policy might be woven. The weight to be placed on each of them is a matter of judgment.'

These five Models show that there were two ways of 'tunnelling through the hump', depending on whether one treated it as a hump of student numbers or a hump of cost. So one could either depress student opportunity and maintain standards, or maintain numbers but – for the time being at any rate – depress standards. Another model canvassed structural changes designed to maintain numbers but relieve the pressure on expenditure – such as two-year courses[9] and deferred

---

[9] An oddity about the proposal for a two-year course which distinguished the Brown Paper from the earlier Treasury thinking on the same idea, was that the authors of the Brown Paper thought it might be appropriate for the *abler* students, on the ground that they

entry, both of which had figured long ago in Treasury thinking during the sessions of the Robbins Committee. Finally the paper offered colourable reasons for supposing that in fact the expected decline in the demand for higher education would not occur at all, so that the apparent 'hump' would be no more than another crest on the upward climb. The whole tone was tentative and helpful, the figures were fairly presented. It produced little effect, and within a year of its publication the Labour Government that had produced it was replaced by the Conservatives.

Modest though the Brown Paper was in manner, it was still infused with the idea – unstated because it was regarded as axiomatic – that it was for Government to plan and finance higher education. Indeed this conviction had grown stronger than ever during the past twenty years. The foundation of a university institution at Buckingham which forswore Government finance was thought of by most people as eccentric, and by many as an act of almost political defiance.

What this approach ignored was the intense competitiveness which exists in a university system, between institutions, between subjects and between individuals. A system of planning which ignores this factor will proceed bumpily and with difficulty. When funds are plentiful, competitiveness, though still present, matters less, for there are consolation prizes for all. But when they become scarce, competitiveness comes into its own.

The last year of the last and fractured quinquennium ended on 31 July 1977. It had been preceded by four years of financing which it would be polite to describe as annual, so frequent were the interruptions, supplementations and adjustments. The UGC fought hard for the continuance of quinquennial settlements, even in modified form, but there was no longer any room in the now uniform public expenditure survey system for exceptions of that old-fashioned sort. All that could be got was what everyone else got, 'planning figures' of diminishing firmness for five years ahead, revised each year.

That final quinquennium ended with a number of students very close to the lower aim set by the UGC after the crisis of 1973 – 272,000. One would like to say that the aims of the Robbins projections were still being maintained. That can be said, and was said at the time, of higher education as a whole, but it was not true for universities taken separately, or indeed of the colleges of education. The total

could get through the work more quickly. The Treasury thought of it as more appropriate for the *less able* students on the ground that they needed, and could absorb, less.

number of 516,000 on the 'Robbins Path' was made up by more than a quarter of a million in a 'public sector' to which the Robbins projection had assigned far fewer.

Of course the number of students in the universities continued to grow substantially during the quinquennium – they increased by more than 30,000; but the academic staff had not increased in proportion. At its beginning they had been 30,000, and at the end 32,209. The great majority of them were between 35 and 50, so despite the vastly increased numbers of students completing their courses with distinction, recruitment was lower than for many years past and the prospect of recovery from the 'dip in quality' of academic staff which the Robbins Committee had foreseen and accepted was still far away.

It is in the light of this that one must look at what had happened to the money. The quinquennial settlement of 1972 had opened with figures of £252m for its first year and £309m for its last.[10] In the outcome the figure for the last year – now in the form of grant plus fees – was well over £600m. This doubling of university costs in monetary terms was entirely due to inflation, and indeed was not inflation's full measure. The staff, it was generally agreed, was being paid on scales less favourable in real terms at the end of the quinquennium than at the beginning. Many economies had been made. But the fact remained that a very considerably smaller amount was being devoted to the universities than had been proposed only five years earlier.

Reviewing the penultimate year of that last quinquennium the UGC wrote words which bring an appropriate end to the main narrative portion of this book:

The year under review [1975–6] marked a decisive down-turn in a process of growth of resources which has continued for twenty years and is unlikely soon to be resumed. Universities are now conscious not only of difficult but of novel problems which cannot be solved by improvisation. At the same time the financial system which permitted and encouraged forward planning has been seriously damaged by successive short-term decisions. As a result there is a deep and damaging sense of uncertainty which can only be removed by the restoration of a longer-term planning horizon.[11]

[10] At the prices of July 1971 taken in *Education: A Framework for Expansion.*
[11] *UGC Annual Survey for 1975–76*, Cmnd 6750, HMSO, paragraph 24.

XIII

Some Conclusions

It is not my intention to describe events after 1978, when my direct experience of university–state relations came to an end, but the existence of a subsequent and cataclysmic period must cast a shadow over any conclusions that can be suggested from what I have said so far.

Looking back at the scene as it was in the 1930s one finds it almost unrecognisable, so many and great have been the changes in the relationship between the universities and the state. But this has not, as might appear at first sight, taken the form of integrating the two more closely. The universities of fifty years ago were very closely integrated with the state as it then was, but in a quite different way; and they formed just as indispensable a part of the framework of national institutions as they do now. The links, however, were personal and social, not bureaucratic or formal. The universities and the machinery of Government in both its political and official aspects formed a kind of continuum, in which only the sketchiest of formality was either expected or required to maintain necessary relationships. This was enormously assisted by the small size of the university world and by its concentration in a comparatively few powerful centres. An obscure and confidential committee was all that was needed to transfer the marginal – but essential – Exchequer subsidy to the institutions in a decorous and impartial way.

Since then universities, though only the greater part of higher education, became a conspicuous feature in the general public landscape. Tens of thousands came to depend on them for a livelihood and hundreds of thousands for their careers or hopes. They became bound up in the public mind with the economic future of the country and with the turbulence of students. Many scholars and scientists found themselves acting on a public stage. The universities became subject not only to speculative comment but to weekly analysis by skilful and articulate commentators, many of whom held university posts themselves. Their staffs become unionised, with all the formality that entails. Gradually the social continuum between the state and the universities which had been the original basis of their financial relationship was replaced by an official system.

Two forces had brought about the expansion to which Robbins gave voice in Britain. One was the need, clearly perceived in the wake of the War, but never wholly satisfied, for graduates – above all for graduates in science and technology. The other was the ineluctable pressure for educational advance from one stage to the next, promoted by the concern (and in some cases the ambition) of parents, teachers and institutions. Both these forces were present in most countries, but in Britain the task of satisfying them was assumed in the years following the War, and by common consent, by the state. This was the unspoken axiom of the Robbins Report.

The formal relationship between the universities and the state which had been inherited from the 1930s was capable of sustaining this expansion so long as the general economy was itself expanding, or was, at any rate, not declining. Indeed the protection it gave to the universities meant that there would be some lag between general stringency and the arrival of pressure on university support. But on the other hand the direct connection between university support and the Exchequer made savings on that account only too attractive as alternatives to savings which might have been much larger but were more difficult to achieve. Once the state had plucked up the courage to reach for the tap it was found to lie remarkably ready to hand.

During the period of expansion the system, large though it was, could be steered by a touch of the tiller here and there – a nudge as it used to be called – and by adding desirable developments in what were thought to be the right places. But no serious thought had ever been given to the possibility that – whether because of shortage of resources or shortage of students – growth might actually have to go into reverse. To have foreseen and provided for such a contingency in, say, 1964 would have seemed not only absurd but in a way morally wrong. Just the same, it is one thing to restrain a growth deemed to be unsound, and quite another actually to demand the excision of established fibre: for the excision had to be done, in the last resort, by the very bodies of which the fibre was a part. The principle of autonomy imposed the act as well as the pains of amputation on the patient himself.

In this situation two schools of thought began to emerge. One said that the state was interfering too much and the UGC had become no more than its agent and catspaw. The other argued that in its policies on higher education the state had drifted rudderless and that more effective leadership by it and by the UGC could have avoided the brutal measures that were ultimately taken. One developed from what I have called the high-church view, the other from the evangelical. When the blow fell in 1981 and recurrent grant was ruthlessly cut, I remember Lord Robbins saying the UGC should simply have passed the percentage on to each university without any attempt to differentiate. But there is no doubt in my own mind that such abdication would have meant the complete collapse of the UGC system, and that selectivity was the only course by which not only its authority but the autonomous identity of each university could have been preserved.

From this point of view the recognisable steps from a continuum to a formal and ultimately adversarial relationship can be seen as inevitable: the formation of the DES and its substitution for the Treasury in relation to the universities; the evanescence of the 'dual Accounting Officer' arrangement; the admittance of parliamentary audit; the assumption of control by the state over fees and over salary settlements; the growth of the UGC secretariat and the bureaucratisation of its procedures;[1] all these were no more than symptoms of the situation under which the state had undertaken the responsibility of meeting the needs identified by the Robbins Report.

But if these movements within the Government machine were inevitable, some important decisions were not, and if they had gone otherwise, the story would have been different.

One of these concerns the historical accident by which the Anderson Committee completed its work on student support which was then built into the fabric in advance of the general survey undertaken by the Robbins Committee. Perhaps if the Robbins Committee had been asked to consider student support as well as the pattern and size of the institutional system, it would have come up with the same answer as the Anderson Committee. But this is far from certain. Lord Robbins was not himself opposed to the concept of student loans. But however

---

[1] It has sometimes been suggested that the calibre of the staff of the UGC declined as original Treasury personnel retired and DES staff took their places. I have always felt that the UGC should be allowed to trawl more widely in Whitehall – and the universities – for its vacancies, and several successful experiments were in fact made in this direction. But I do not think (and in practice the Secretary of the UGC was in a position to veto any appointment proposed by the DES) that there was any loss of calibre at senior levels. The notion almost certainly derives from the three-fold expansion of the UGC during the Wolfenden era, which necessarily brought in more officers at lower ranks, to whom much business was devolved which would have been dealt with at senior levels in earlier days.

that may be, at least parliament and public would have been presented with an integrated picture.[2]

The second, and more serious, of the decisions which could have gone otherwise concerned the local authority area of higher education. On this issue the Robbins Report, with its proposal for an overarching Higher Education Commission, offered an escape. The loss of that opportunity is attributable to institutional power. On the one hand the existing universities wished to see the survival of the UGC they knew, with its mission to them and any that might be promoted to join them. On the other hand the local authorities, the educational interests and the Education Departments were unwilling to yield up to a Commission the institutions that remained within their control. Two competing, uncoordinated and jealous sectors was the unhappy result.

The one time at which this could have been avoided was in the immediate aftermath of the Robbins Report when all was fluid. Time was lacking, and a general election was in the air. But if it had been done, not only would the sorrows of binarism have been avoided but the new Commission would have had far more weight in Whitehall than the UGC as it emerged into the new world trying to look as like its old self as possible.

Leadership and policy were thus scattered and dispersed. The Secretary of State and his Department were forbidden by convention and policy from intervention but were under constant pressure to intervene: the UGC covered only part of the field, with a strict tradition of respecting the autonomy of institutions within it; and it took twenty years to produce anything resembling effective coordination of the local institutions themselves, let alone of the two 'sectors'. The arithmetic of the Robbins Report so far as it concerned 'sectors' was from that moment irrelevant, and university numbers became a matter of departmental decision.

The failure at the time of the Robbins Report or very soon afterwards to consider the terms of service for the enormous increase of staff that was planned constitutes another missed opportunity. The essential guarantees of professional freedom and the problem of combining rapid

---

[2] There is an interesting discussion of loan finance in the Robbins Report (paragraphs 641 to 647) which makes it clear that the Committee was divided on the issue. Their conclusion – to go on with the Anderson system for the time being but to consider introducing loans later – meant that any later examinations of the question revealed an enormous initial cost which was unacceptable.

expansion with maintenance of quality and future opportunity for the ablest could then have had authoritative and lasting solutions. As it was, the tradition of tenure was assumed almost without discussion, with many unhappy results for the future.

Finally there were the two mistakes that must be laid at the door of the Robbins Committee itself: the failure to take account of medical education and the overprovision for science, both of which I have discussed earlier. Medical education was important because of its enormous potential cost and its manifest social implications; the initial overprovision for science led not only to undue expenditure but to overcrowding and lack of opportunity in the arts, a decline of standards in some science entries, and an addition to the problem of overseas students which had not been foreseen. If in the early sixties some of the capital that was spent on science buildings had gone to medical buildings and the growth of science been matured first in the schools much expense would have been saved and some loss of confidence avoided. Priority, however, was given to science in higher education.

The tables in Appendix I show how grievously the plan for growth in numbers in science and technology was disappointed, and the main reason why this happened. But the shortfall of 83,000 students of those subjects in 1980 feebly reflects the broader picture. The accumulated deficits of previous years since 1962 have come to about 150,000 newly qualified scientists and technologists, with social, industrial and international consequences of a most far-reaching kind which will be felt for many years to come. If, during the next twenty years, the deficit continues at the rate it reached in 1980 its total since the Robbins Report will come to something like three-quarters of a million. While that is unlikely to happen, the calculation illustrates the scale of the problem; and it should be remembered that it is wholly related to what the Robbins Committee projected. It allows for no addition to the total number of university students or for the increased pace of scientific and technological advance.

The other causes which contributed to the reversals of the late seventies and early eighties were not foreseeable, and no committee, Minister or civil servant could have provided against them. They were two in number. The first was the gathering pace of inflation which eroded and finally destroyed the quinquennial planning horizon and reduced managements at every level to a condition of perpetual crisis and fear of worse to come. This was also the prime reason for the appearance of state intervention in circumstances where no administrative device could prevent an item of expenditure as large as the university vote from being included in the successive jerks and convulsions that afflicted financial policy at the centre.

The other is less easy to define. The Robbins arithmetic engendered the habit of thinking in terms of student numbers as the main determinant of planning for the total system, the distribution between main subject areas, and the allocation to institutions. Finance, whether in the form of recurrent grant or of capital expenditure to create new capacity, came second. Yet in the end it was resources, not students, that were in the gift of the Exchequer.

Pressure for more students at a lower unit cost therefore became the inevitable if unspoken policy of all Secretaries of State, and, as the universities began to lose popularity during the later sixties, this policy gained wider support and universities were placed on the defensive.

That the state should ultimately determine the resources it will devote to higher education seems to me beyond dispute; but I am far from sure that the setting of the fraction of the population which ought to receive higher education is a proper function of central authority; and I am still more doubtful whether such a function is appropriate in respect of particular 'sectors', subject groups or institutions. The aid of the state should certainly be withheld from institutions which either fail to attract students in sufficient numbers, or so stretch their staff and resources that they unacceptably dilute the quality of what they offer. But however that may be, the labour and anxiety put into the setting of student 'targets' do not seem to have been justified by the outcome, as the following figures show.

At the time of the Robbins Committee (1961–2) there were 113,000 students in the universities. For the short term (1967–8) the Report proposed 153,000, and for the long term (1980–1) 346,000. The first of these was more than attained – it turned out to be 200,000, despite the fact that the element for science and technology fell considerably below what the Report had recommended both proportionately and absolutely. In the longer term the Robbins proposal for university numbers was not reached: it turned out to be 290,000, though the total for higher education as a whole was more than made up by the expansion of the polytechnics. In the intervening years the 'target' for universities had been hoisted as high as 375,000 (*Education: A Framework for Expansion*, 1972), and even in 1978 was placed at 310,000 (*Higher Education into the 1990s*).

In the middle of this turbulent sea the UGC was expected to float. It was to safeguard the universities and respond to the needs of Governments, acting as a source of wisdom for both, yet equipped with little formal authority. Its more open admonitions, whether they concerned Russian studies, libraries or mergers of facilities, were addressed to universities and met with resistance – in some cases with defiance. Its more covert protests, which were addressed to Governments and usually concerned sudden reductions in resources or equally sudden alterations in the financial arrangements, were partially successful, but as time passed they were increasingly met by sorrowful regrets either that circumstances which were outside the control of the DES, or that consequences for other sectors of higher education, prevented any positive answer. What had been claimed as the UGC's strengths tended to become its weaknesses. At the centre of its philosophy was the doctrine that it did not run the universities. But if it did not, the outsider kept saying, what does?

It was the reverse of Baldwin's famous epigram on the press: responsibility without power. The Chairman and the Secretary found themselves in the sixties habitually denying their power when they spoke to university audiences, and emphasising the managerial responsibilities of universities; while implying – without actually asserting – to Government and Parliament that persuasion, influence, financial pressure could be exerted on the universities to maintain orderly progress. But in the seventies, and still more in the eighties, the method of dealing with this dilemma altered. It began to be said with increasing emphasis by the UGC that failure to follow its guidance could only place the universities in less sympathetic hands, for in everything that truly mattered about university autonomy the UGC was as deeply committed as the highest-church college in Oxford or Cambridge.

So far I have been concerned in this chapter to dwell on a darker side and attribute reasons for the transition from euphoria to discontent which marked these eighteen years. But in a way that transition only marks a much wider transition in national and even in world affairs. That mood of euphoria broke in the later sixties, and student revolt was the foam on the crest of the wave. There was a better side, in which the universities, the UGC and even the DES can claim a share.

The pledges given by the Government in the wake of the Robbins Report for the period down to 1973–4 were more than fulfilled, with a capital endowment and a maintenance of staffing that in no way fell short of traditional measurements; and the Robbins projection for

1980–1, before which the Government of 1963 had hesitated, was nearly achieved for higher education as a whole, despite the need to reduce the programme of teacher training, which Robbins did not allow for. The full increase of university numbers was not achieved, but it did not fall very far short.

Taking a broad view it cannot be said that in achieving this there was much serious encroachment on university autonomy – the fee question being the main exception. This may seem more difficult to accept, but one should remember the replacement of a social continuum by a bureaucratic system which marks the period. A line came to be drawn between the universities and Government which nobody had felt to be there before – not at any rate since King James II sought to impose his choice of President on the Fellows of Magdalen.

The UGC sustained the notion of continuum for a very long time. Its daily life – or rather the life of the Chairman and in a measure the Secretary and senior officials – was much taken up during the period of which I speak by consultations about university problems which were not financial, and much advice which was independent but in no way binding was the result. The UGC became expert in launching small but strategic initiatives – pump-priming grants for technology, industrial liaison officers, allocations to business studies, four-year, high-calibre engineering courses, special grants for advanced study in the humanities.

And even as the system became more encrusted by bureaucratic barnacles – many of them at the behest of the Public Accounts Committee – it never reached the point at which the Secretary could dream of writing, as his counterpart in democratic France had written on a file seeking travelling expenses for a group of university Rectors to attend a conference abroad:

Non. Ces Messieurs voyagent trop.

I have stressed the failure of the programme to fulfil expectations in science and technology, and the fact that this was primarily due to the shortage of women students in these subjects. But the counterpart to this is the immense success of the programme in advancing the position of women in society. It sounds a feeble expression of this to say that the proportion of women students in the higher education system as a whole (including teacher training, where even in 1962 they constituted a majority) rose over the eighteen years from $31\frac{1}{2}$ per cent to over 40 per cent. The total in the last year of the eighteen was nearly three times as large as in the first. In many arts and social science departments women students are now a majority. Nearly half the medical students are women and the quotas on women medical students (in some cases the absolute bans) are a remote memory. At Oxford and Cambridge the main preoccupation became the preservation of a handful of colleges where women who wished to do so could have an establishment to themselves. Altogether, between 1962 and 1980 at least one million women graduated.

The notion that universities are somehow apart from the workaday world (unlike other institutions of higher education) has been nourished by literature and has a foundation in the professional detachment and mutual esteem of university people. Just the same, it is an illusion. Far from being separated from the currents of ordinary life, universities are almost excessively sensitive to them and reflect them in a thousand ways. The university world is competitive for funds, for students and for reputation, as well as for religion and good learning. If these rewards are in prospect there is no need to kick universities into a pattern amid cries for responsiveness and relevance. Subject to certain lags as opinion changes course, a nation will get what it needs from its universities if funds, students and reputation are allowed them.

But it cannot be denied that in the period from 1960 to 1978 planning for higher education inside and outside the institutions – and predominantly outside – suffered from flaws of which perhaps the greatest was hesitation between the well-tried and by then well-loved landscape and the attractions of adventure. Both had their claims in those years, but I heard with a chill a distinguished business man declaring in the face of a long list of bids from universities to develop business studies that since neither Oxford nor Cambridge was among them he for one saw no point in continuing the discussion.

Earlier chapters have pointed out failures and triumphs in the Robbins chapter of the history of the universities. The chapter is now closed, primarily because the celebrated 'Robbins principle' has itself ceased to provide an adequate beacon.[3] The word 'qualified' in the famous formula 'all those who are qualified by ability and attainment'

---

[3] It is a frequent error to suppose that the 'Robbins principle' means that all those achieving a specific level of achievement in school examinations should be found a place somewhere in the system if they wish for it. This is not the case, and was never stated to be so. It is irreconcilable with the right of institutions and departments within them to decide their own requirements for admission, in terms of both subjects and attainment. Such decisions must obviously take into account, among other factors, the facilities available at that particular place and the range of quality in the candidates for them.

acquired definition only because the Committee took the broad level of admission of 1962 as 'qualified' and then enlarged future numbers to allow for larger age-groups and a developing school system producing more candidates at that level. Thus, although it implied no reduction in standards, it did imply a very large expansion of the institutions. But the institutions, once enlarged, could hardly be expected to contract, even if changes in demography made this theoretically desirable to maintain the standards of 1962. So at the turn of the decade the system was faced with the question –as yet unresolved – of substituting something else for 'qualified by the standards of 1962'.

Throughout the period, and indeed after it had ended, decision on this has been obscured and discussion diverted by the priority given to structural questions, as against those of substance. Much of the debate has been carried on as if structures and methods of finance were the keys to effective teaching and research. It is true that the Robbins Committee set a fashion for this by its own emphasis on structure, but it also saw higher education as a larger unity within which many institutions of different kinds could flourish under the broad tree of autonomy. Later developments, especially the binarist approach enunciated by Crosland, impaired this vision and diverted effort from the real objectives.

The state and the universities are like a discontented couple who cannot live without each other: he rich, busy, self-important, preoccupied with the office; she proud, independent and in her own opinion beautiful. The state–husband will always complain about her extravagance and inconstancy, and the university–wife will endlessly denounce his stinginess, jealousy and philistinism. Her parting words in the endlessly renewed argument will be that she knows he has a mistress – 'and very common she is'. But they would not dream of parting: because of the children.

Appendix I

Programme and Performance

The following four tables compare a number of aspects of the proposals of the Robbins Committee in terms of full-time student numbers down to 1980 with the outcome in that year. The first line of each table gives the 1962 position as stated in the Robbins Report. Subsequent lines show (or in some cases estimate) the increases proposed in the Report, and the last two lines give the numbers actually achieved in 1980 and thus the difference between programme and performance. The 1980 figures are taken from *Statistics of Education* for that year.

All the figures refer to full-time students at degree level (or equivalent) and above, and include full-time students at advanced level in further education. Overseas students, who formed between 9 and 12 per cent of the whole student body at different times during the period, are included. Since part-time students are not included the tables do not show the contribution of the Open University.

The figures are for Great Britain, and do not include Northern Ireland.

Table 1 gives the overall picture and is divided by 'sectors', namely the institutions receiving support from the UGC on the one hand, and all the rest receiving support from public funds on the other. I have counted the contribution of the colleges of advanced technology in the 'university sector' figures for 1962, though they did not join the UGC Grant List until afterwards. The 'public sector' institutions include polytechnics, other further education institutions offering advanced courses, colleges of education in England, Scotland and Wales, Central Institutions in Scotland, and the two specialised higher educational institutions still financed by the Department of Education and Science – the Royal College of Art and the Cranfield Institute.

The table shows that overall performance came within 6 per cent of programme, and at mid-term considerably exceeded it. But the later tables qualify this conclusion in important respects, and Table 1 itself shows that as between the 'sectors' the programme was not achieved in the way the Robbins Report proposed. The last line of the table does not indicate a failure on the part of the UGC institutions to achieve the Robbins objective, but reflects the subsequent decision to develop further education on a much larger scale than the Robbins Report had proposed, with a consequent redistribution of both numbers and resources.

Table 2 contrasts the proposed and actual expansion of student numbers in science/technology and in 'other subjects' taken as a whole. The estimating principle is shown as a note to the table. The short-hand 'science/technology' is taken as including mathematics, physics, chemistry, biology and all forms of engineering and computer studies, but excludes medicine, dentistry and veterinary studies.

The table shows how grievously (by about 25 per cent) the numbers fell short in science/technology over the twenty-year period, and how, despite the cut-back in teacher training, 'other subjects' exceeded the objective by about 17 per cent in compensation. These 'other subjects' include business studies, economics and medi-

169

cine as well as the humanities, and it should be noted that, because of the length of the medical course, medical students bulk larger *in any given year* in relation to 'opportunity' at one end or graduate output at the other, than most other groups.

Table 3 shows the intended and actual distribution of places between the sexes, so far as the former can be estimated from the Report. Broadly speaking, over the twenty-year period, the number of women students trebled, and that of men doubled, so that women rose from just over 30 per cent of the student body to more than 40 per cent. This growth, however, was mainly in non-science subjects, as is shown by Table 4 which contrasts the growth in science/technology numbers as between the sexes. It shows that the expansion came very near the objective in respect of men (though here students from overseas played an important part), so that almost the whole of the short-fall in science/technology shown in Table 3 is attributable to the absence of the women students who had been hoped for. The number of women students in science/technology did indeed more than double over the period, but the base in 1962 was so low that this made little difference. The prognostications required it to expand by more than eight times.

Table I   Development of the 'sectors' 1962–80, Great Britain
(000s full-time students)

	UGC institutions	'Public sector' institutions	Total
1 Actual 1962	130	86	216
2 Addition for 1967 proposed by Robbins Committee	67	45	112
3 Total (1) + (2)	197	131	328
4 Actual 1967	200	179	379
5 Further addition proposed by Robbins Committee for 1980	149	81	230
6 Robbins proposal for 1980 ((3)+ (5))	346	212	558
7 Actual 1980	301	223	524
8 Difference between programme and performance	−45	+11	−34

Source: Robbins Report and *Statistics of Education.*
Notes
(1) All the entries in the first column include the colleges of advanced technology, though they did not in fact become universities until 1964.
(2) The entries in the second column bring together further education to advanced level in England and Wales and the equivalent in Scotland, and teacher training in Great Britain as a whole. Lines 2, 6 and 7 should be read with the important reservations that (i) the Robbins Report much overstated the need for teacher training, and (ii) further education expanded far more quickly than the Robbins Committee had proposed. While these departures in opposite directions almost cancel each other out, the components of the figures 212 in line 6 and 223 in line 7 are very different.
(3) Line 7 includes advanced courses.

Table 2 Science/technology contrasted with all other subjects, Great Britain
(000s full-time students)

	UGC institutions		'Public sector' institutions		Totals all institutions		Grand total all institutions, all subjects
	Science/ technology	Other subjects	Science/ technology	Other subjects	Science/ technology	Other subjects	
1 Actual 1962	59	71	26	60	85	131	216
2 Addition to 1980 proposed by Robbins Committee	136	80	38	88	174	168	342
3 Robbins proposal for 1980 ((1) + (2))	195	151	64	148	259	299	558
4 Actual 1980	112	188	64	160	176	348	524
5 Difference between programme and performance	−83	+37	nil	+12	−83	+49	−34

Notes

(1) Lines 2 and 3 have been estimated on the basis that the Robbins Committee intended about two-thirds of the additional places which they proposed in universities and further education should go to science/technology; and that in teacher training colleges the balance of subjects should remain unchanged.

(2) Line 5 should be read bearing in mind that the Robbins 'target' for further education, which envisaged successive transfers of further education institution to the 'university sector', was almost at once superseded by the 'binarist' policy of developing the 'public sector' separately.

(3) Line 4 includes advanced courses.

Table 3　Male and female students at degree and advanced level, all
subjects and all types of institution in Great Britain
(000s full-time students)

	Women	Men	Total
1 Actual 1962	68	148	216
2 Addition to 1980 proposed by Robbins Committee	185	157	342
3 Robbins proposal for 1980 ((1) + (2))	253	305	558
4 Actual 1980	214	310	524
5 Difference between programme and performance	−39	+5	−34

Notes
(1) The additional places in line 2 have been estimated on the basis that the additions assigned by Robbins to the universities and further education were to be equally divided between the sexes, but that two-thirds of the extra places assigned to teacher training would be filled by women. Although the rundown of teacher training was largely compensated by the development of further education institutions, the difference between lines 3 and 4 for women students should be read with this in mind.
(2) Line 4 includes advanced courses.

Table 4　Science/technology at degree or advanced level, distribution
between male and female students, all types of institution in
Great Britain
(000s full-time students)

	Women	Men	Total
1 Actual 1962	12	73	85
2 Addition to 1980 estimated by reference to Robbins Report	87	87	174
3 Estimated target for 1980 on basis of Robbins Report ((1) + (2))	99	160	259
4 Actual 1980	28	148	176
5 Difference between programme and performance ((3) − (4))	−71	−12	−83

Appendix II

Principal Office-Holders in Whitehall Concerned with Universities 1960–80

1. Senior Ministers

All these had seats in the Cabinet. The first two were Chancellors of the Exchequer. Lord Hailsham exercised his responsibility first as Lord President of the Council and Minister for Science, then as Secretary of State for Education and Science, being the first Minister to hold that office, which was occupied by all his successors in this list. The Secretaries of State for Scotland exercise some statutory responsibilities for some universities in Scotland, and are, of course, responsible for higher education in Scotland otherwise than in universities, but they are not included here. The dates in brackets relate to the period of responsibility for university matters, not tenure of the office.

Selwyn Lloyd (to 1963)
Reginald Maudling (1963)
Quintin Hogg, Lord Hailsham (1963–4)
Michael Stewart (1964)
Anthony Crosland (1964–8)
Patrick Gordon-Walker (1968)
Edward Short (1968–70)
Margaret Thatcher (1970–4)
Reginald Prentice (1974–5)
Frederick Mulley (1975–6)
Shirley Williams (1976–9)
Mark Carlisle (1979–81)

2. Other Ministers

The practice with these appointments varied considerably. The first three in the list held Cabinet rank. Of the others some held the rank of Minister of State (this was normal under Labour administrations) others that of Parliamentary Under-Secretary. Often they had other responsibilities within the Department besides higher education. Between 1972 and 1974 the Secretary of State did not delegate the responsibility for universities, but performed it herself.

Henry Brooke (Chief Secretary to the Treasury, to 1962)
John Boyd-Carpenter (Chief Secretary to the Treasury, 1962–3)
Edward Boyle (Minister of State, 1963–4)
Vivian Bowden, Lord Bowden (Minister of State, 1964–5)
Jennie Lee (Parliamentary Under-Secretary 1965–7, Minister of State, 1967–70)*
Reginald Prentice (Minister of State, 1965–7)
Shirley Williams (Minister of State, 1967–9)

* Miss Lee's university responsibilities related only to the Open University

Appendix II

Gerald Fowler (Minister of State, 1969–70)
W. R. van Straubenzee (Parliamentary Under-Secretary, 1970–2)
Gerald Fowler (Minister of State, 1974)
Norman Crowther-Hunt, Lord Crowther-Hunt (Minister of State, 1974–6)
Gerald Fowler (Minister of State, 1976)
Gordon Oakes (Minister of State, 1976–9)

3. Permanent Secretaries

These held office under various titles, and the test for inclusion in this list is the responsibility as Accounting Officer for the University Vote between the dates shown.

Sir Richard Clarke (Second Secretary to the Treasury; to 1963)
Sir Maurice Dean (Second Secretary to the Treasury and Joint Permanent Under-Secretary to the DES, 1963–4)
Sir Bruce Fraser (Joint Permanent Under-Secretary to the DES, 1964–5)
Sir Herbert Andrew (Permanent Under-Secretary to the DES, 1965–70)
Sir William Pile (Permanent Under-Secretary to the DES, 1970–6)
Sir James Hamilton (Permanent Under-Secretary to the DES, 1976–83)

4. Deputy Secretaries DES

From 1965, when the Joint Accounting Officer arrangement came to an end, work in the DES was divided under the Permanent Under-Secretary into a number of Deputy Secretary 'charges', of which one was concerned with higher education on both sides of the binary divide.

Sir Toby Weaver (1965–71)
Edward Simpson (1971–4)
Alan Thompson (1975–80)

5. 'Desk Officers' concerned with Universities

In the Treasury relations with the UGC were among the responsibilities of SS Division, headed by an undersecretary. On the formation of the DES they were assigned to a new branch, also headed by an undersecretary, which took over, in addition, certain other responsibilities either inherited from the Treasury (such as the British Academy) or already part of the old Ministry of Education, notably student awards and a number of direct grant institutions of higher education. The branch has had a succession of titles, but its responsibilities have remained more or less the same.

J. A. C. Robertson (Treasury Head of SS, 1960–2)
Samuel Goldman (Treasury Head of SS, 1962)
H. A. Harding (Treasury Head of SS, 1962–4)
John Carswell (DES, 1964–7)
Ronald Guppy (1967–9)
Ralph Toomey (1969–78)

174

6. University Grants Committee

(1) Chairmen. Until 1963 the Chairman, who is technically a civil servant, was appointed by the Chancellor of the Exchequer. From that time onwards he has been appointed by the Secretary of State for Education and Science after consultation with the Secretaries of State for Scotland and for Wales and after receiving the approval of the Prime Minister. The term is for five years and is renewable, but no Chairman has served for more than ten years, though Sir Keith Murray was offered a third term.

Sir Keith Murray (1953–63)
Sir John Wolfenden (1963–8)
Sir Kenneth Berrill (1969–73)
Sir Frederick Dainton (1973–8)
Sir Edward Parkes (1978–83)

(2) Secretaries. The Secretary is a civil servant appointed by the responsible Minister with the approval of the Prime Minister.

Sir Edward Hale (1954–8; original Department Treasury)
Sir Cecil Syers (1958–63; original Department Dominions Office)
E. R. Copleston (1963–9; original Department Treasury)
Ralph Fletcher (1970–3; original Department Education)
John Carswell (1974–7; original Department National Insurance)
Geoffrey Cockerill (1977–82; original Department Education)

(3) Undersecretaries. Until 1964, and after 1971, there was one post at this rank in the UGC. Between those dates there were two. After 1982 there were none. This bears a close relationship with the pace of university growth.

E. R. Copleston (1963; afterwards Secretary; formerly Treasury)
Richard Griffiths (1963–70; formerly Treasury and Admiralty)
Alan Thompson (1964–8; formerly Education)
Geoffrey Caston (1970–2; formerly Colonial Office, Ministry of Overseas Development, and Education)
E. St G. Moss (1971–8; formerly Defence and Education)

Of the ten senior officials of the UGC listed above, four had no previous experience of Education Departments; three had had their main experience in non-educational departments; and three had served only in the Ministry of Education. Only one continued in the civil service after service with the UGC.

Over the twenty years the average duration for a political appointment was 1.7 years; and for an official appointment 3.7 years.

How to Count Universities

There are two different ways of reckoning the number of universities in this country, and therefore of deciding what constitutes 'the universities'. The first is to count the number of teaching institutions that have, by charter, the right to grant degrees or their equivalent. The second is to count the number of institutions on the grant list of the University Grants Committee. The results are by no means the same.

On the first criterion there are forty-six universities in Great Britain, including the Open University, the University College of Buckingham, the Cranfield Institute, and the Royal College of Art.

It is usually said, by reference to the UGC grant list that there are forty-three universities because one should include the University of Manchester Institute of Science and Technology (which is formally part of the University of Manchester) as in effect a separate institution, and the two business schools of Manchester and London, one of which is, and the other is not, formally a part of the University of the city where it is located. All three of these receive grant directly from the UGC. And one should omit the Open University (though it, unlike the two business schools, has a seat on the Committee of Vice-Chancellors and Principals), Buckingham, Cranfield, and the Royal College of Art.

The UGC grant list, however, comprises fifty-two institutions, since it also treats each of the eight components of the University of Wales (including its Registry) separately, and the UGC *indicates*, in its grant to the University of London, the amount that should be reserved for Imperial College.

These figures do not take account of the two university institutions in Northern Ireland, on whose grants the UGC advises, and who have seats on the CVCP. So perhaps, for the United Kingdom, one should say fifty-four.

The number of institutions *visited* by the UGC is much larger than its grant list, and amounts to over seventy because of the inclusion of all the separate Schools and Institutes of the University of London in the scope of visitation.

Index

Index

Index

quinquennial system (*contd.*)
  1967–72, 92, 112, 135
  1972–77, 141, 144, 145, 157–8, 163
  see also recurrent grant

rates, on universities, 108–10
Reagan, Ronald, 123, 124
recurrent grant
  principles, 84–5
  average per student, 97, 102, 141
  adjustment for fee income, 111, 153–5
  see also quinquennial system
'redbrick' universities, 3–5, 71, 138
Reid, William, 29
research councils, 58–60, 83, 107–8, 113
residence of students, 4, 40–2, 62, 82, 95, 121,
  141, 152
Rhodesia, 124
Robbins Committee (The Committee on Higher
  Education), 18, 26, 27–37, 38
  appointment and terms of reference, 19, 22, 25,
  27, 68
  membership, 29–33
  secretariat, 28–9
  Report of, 37, 38–51, 58, 59, 119
    underlying principle, 38–9, 130, 140, 144,
    147, 167–8
    structural proposals, 52–5, 168
    student support, 23, 162
    university fees, 46–7, 111–12
    institutional autonomy, 76, 86, 88, 121
    UGC principle, supports, 114, 133, 137
    elevated language, 124
    public impact, 97
    projections of student places, 42–3, 143,
    157–8
    student militancy and, 120, 129
    problems of implementing, 60–3, 67, 70–2
Robbins, Lord
  character and outlook, 27–28, 29, 31–32, 111
  binarism, disapproval of, 124
  Chairman of the Court of LSE, 125
  student loans, views on, 161
  opinion of, in 1981 161
Robens of Wolsingham, Lord, 63
Roberston, J.A.C., 16
'ROSLA' (Raising of School Leaving Age) 23
Ross, Philip, 29
Royal College of Art, 53, 138
Royal Commissions, 27, 79
Rucker, Sir Arthur, 86
Ruskin College, 30

St Andrews, University of, 6, 11, 15, 34, 132
salaries of university teachers, 17, 36, 98–100, 134,
  145, 148–50, 161
Salford, University of, 61
  see also colleges of advanced technology
science and technology,
  in pre-war universities, 7–8
  responsibility of the Treasury for, 10
  Robbins report emphasises, 44–5, 51
  reorganization of government support for, 58–9
  Mr Wilson's enthusiasm for, 65
  balance of students in, 85
  empty places in, Dainton inquiry about, 103–5
  shortfall of student numbers in, 160, 163, 164,
  166
Scientific and Industrial Research, Department of,
  58
Scotland
  universities in, 3, 4, 50, 60, 61
  further education in, 74, 138

see also Scottish Education Department *and*
  devolution
Scottish Education Department, 19, 28, 53, 76–7
Shearman, H.C., 30–1, 52–3, 73
Shelley, Percy Bysshe, 127
Short, the rt. hon. Edward, 131
Simpson, Edward, 141
'SISTERS' (Special Institutions of Scientific and
  Technological Education and Research),
  60, 71, 78
Skidmore, David, 58
Sloman, Professor Albert, 135
Smieton, Dame Mary, 131
Snow, Lord, 68
Social Science Research Council, 59
Southall, R.B., 31
staff
  academic
    numbers, 1, 158
    pre-war standing, 4–5, 7
    post-war expansion, 48–9, 62, 127
    superannuation, reform of, 100
    see also salaries
  non-academic, 63–4, 101–2, 134
Stewart, the rt. hon. Michael, 66
Stirling, University of, 61, 62, 129, 135
student militancy, 119–30
  sources, 119–22
  tactics, 121, 122, 124, 125
  public reactions to, 126, 140
  absence of comment by UGC on, 135
  locations, 135–6, 159
  decline, 144
student support
  basis of, established, 23–5, 40–1, 161
  local authorities and, 71
  adjustment, liability to, 113
  nature of, disputed, 120
  NUS and, 24, 122
  loans, 24, 161
  see also Anderson Committee
student unions, 127–8
students
  numbers of, proposed and achieved, 1, 14, 17,
  18, 25, 39, 42–3, 44, 45, 73–4, 92, 132, 140,
  141–2, 136, 147, 156–7, 164
  selection, 6, 121
  family background, 128
  average cost, 132
  representation on university bodies, 126–7
Sussex, University of, 62, 135
Syers, Sir Cecil, 18

technical colleges, 20, 45, 50, 70–4, 141–2, 148–9
  see also colleges of advanced technology
Technology, Ministry of, 67, 68
Teesside, proposed institute at, 61
TGWU (Transport and General Workers' Union),
  101, 149
Thatcher, the rt. hon. Margaret, 92, 131, 139, 156
Thomson, Sir J.J., 2
Todd, Lord, 48
Times Higher Educational Supplement, The, 75, 90
Tolkien, J.R.R., 2
Treasury, HM
  university grant, direct responsibility for,
  10–15, 68, 86, 87
  Robbins Committee and, 16–29, 34–6, 47, 112,
  156
  relinquishes direct responsibility for university
  grant, 54–5, 58
  subsequent behaviour, 79, 96, 129, 146, 154
Trevelyan, G.M., 2
Turvey, Ralph, 29

180

Index